Teaching
for Spiritual Formation

Teaching
for Spiritual Formation

*A Patristic Approach to Christian Education
in a Convulsed Age*

KYLE R. HUGHES

Foreword by David I. Smith

CASCADE *Books* · Eugene, Oregon

TEACHING FOR SPIRITUAL FORMATION
A Patristic Approach to Christian Education in a Convulsed Age

Cascade Books
An Imprint of Wipf and Stock Publishers
199 W. 8th Ave., Suite 3
Eugene, OR 97401

www.wipfandstock.com

PAPERBACK ISBN: 978-1-7252-8123-3
HARDCOVER ISBN: 978-1-7252-8124-0
EBOOK ISBN: 978-1-7252-8125-7

Cataloguing-in-Publication data:

Names: Hughes, Kyle R., author. | Smith, David I., foreword.

Title: Teaching for spiritual formation : a patristic approach to Christian education in a convulsed age / Kyle R. Hughes ; foreword by David I. Smith.

Description: Eugene, OR : Cascade Books, 2022 | Includes bibliographical references and index.

Identifiers: ISBN 978-1-7252-8123-3 (paperback) | ISBN 978-1-7252-8124-0 (hardcover) | ISBN 978-1-7252-8125-7 (ebook)

Subjects: LCSH: Christian education—Study and teaching. | Spiritual formation—Study and teaching.

Classification: BV1471.3 .H84 2022 (paperback) | BV1471.3 .H84 (ebook)

12/23/21

For my grandparents,
Harold and Anne Hughes

Almighty God, by your gift alone we come to wisdom and true understanding: Look with favor, we pray, on our universities, colleges, and schools, that knowledge may be increased among us, and wholesome learning flourish and abound. Bless those who teach and those who learn; and grant that in humility of heart they may ever look to you, the fountain of all wisdom; through Jesus Christ our Lord. Amen.

Book of Common Prayer (2019)

Contents

Foreword

Seeking Conversations with Strangers

Christians who work in education live amid a variety of tensions, real and imagined. One tension seems particularly pertinent to the book that you have just commenced reading. (If, that is, you started at the very beginning. Which, as the book is suggesting, is a very good place to start.)

As members of the Christian church, Christians find themselves belonging to a communion of saints that stretches not only across the world, spanning cultural, ethnic, and political boundaries, but also across time. As compelling as the concerns of the present moment might be, it still matters for the Christian church what Augustine thought about sin, what Luther said about Romans, how Wesley understood sanctification, how the church fathers practiced prayer. Christians do not do theology (at least theology that has much merit) as if folks discovered God last week and the first good thinkers arrived a day or two later. Christians are part of a long conversation unfolding across time amid the communion of saints. More recent is not automatically better. As those who affirm the authority of Scriptures written many centuries ago, Christians have a pretty basic reason for affirming that vital wisdom and compelling direction can come from ancient sources.

As members of the education profession, Christians find themselves in a current thought-world in which decisions are supposed to be data-driven and data comes from the social sciences. Keeping up with the latest findings, methods, and devices is part of professional competence. Ongoing research publications tell us, for instance, that we should teach to particular learning styles or multiple intelligences, and then a decade or two later fresh research publications unveil the lack of solid evidence that these are actually valid; teachers are encouraged to adjust accordingly. After all, there is a great deal at stake in children's education. Why rely on strategies that are grounded mainly in habit and guesswork if fresh findings might show us that something else works better? In this realm, it does not seem as if ancient sources have much to offer. The tendency to read those ancient sources as if they were only talking about narrowly theological matters adds to the challenge. The church fathers might be a good source of prayer fodder, but what could they possibly say about teaching and learning?

Despite appearances, the contrast between these two worlds is not as stark as it may seem. Research can valuably inform our teaching, but it rarely, if ever, can tell us exactly what to do. Empirical research itself depends on ideas and values that come from beyond its scope. Measuring does not get us very far if we have started with bad questions or poorly formed assumptions about what needs measuring or what might count as evidence. Even the best data is of only partial value if it misses the heart of what we are trying to do. Perhaps most importantly, the claim that we are educating children implies a claim that we are somehow making things better, helping them to become better than they would have been without our intervention. "Better" is a value judgment that requires a conception of the good and enough wisdom to see how it might play out in learning. Claiming that a strategy "works better" only makes sense if it is backed up by an idea of what kind of good we are trying to achieve: better for what, and why? Talking well about education includes ideas like assessment, outcomes, and cognitive development but at least as urgently needs ideas like justice, beauty, formation, and hope.

At this point Christians ought to become wary: if, as Scripture warns, the human heart is deceitful, then idolizing either the latest ideas or the ones of a generation ago or any other arbitrary point in the past becomes problematic. Truth is not tied to a particular decade. People did not start being sinners or making self-serving assumptions a few years back (or stop last Christmas). Neither the present nor the past offers us a golden ticket to a perfect classroom or a pristine grasp on things. There is room for repentance in our best ideas.

Yet here the voices of those from a different time and place can be peculiarly helpful. Scripture instructs us to avoid conforming to the pattern of this world, a tricky instruction indeed given that the pattern of our current world has shaped our perceptions, our judgments, our sense of what is possible and viable and valuable. A voice from outside our particular fish bowl (perhaps, say, one from the early years of the Christian church) has potential to help us. Not because what it says will be automatically right, for other times and places have had their own failings and idolatries. But because there is a chance that it is asking questions we might have missed, probing at problems that we have ignored, making connections that slip beneath our own radar. Perhaps its strengths and weaknesses don't mesh with ours, and that might help us to see. In communion with others, precisely others who are not ourselves, we might make headway in learning how to repent, how to seek truth, how to teach and learn in ways that love our students as ourselves.

I think that this is an important part of the service that Kyle Hughes offers in this book. He invites us to spend time in the company of the church fathers, people who, after all, thought and wrote well enough about being Christian that they are still in print and still discussed almost two millennia later. He invites us to read them not just for prayer tips but to get a sense of how they might have imagined the task of learning, the wisdom of teaching, what it means to grow and help others to grow. And he asks us not to replace some current surefire recipe with some hoary old one (solve all your teaching problems with this one second-century trick!) but to tackle the more patient task of seeking wisdom to inform our work. If we are to sustain wisdom in teaching, we need more conversations like this, thoughtful conversations with the best of those who have taught before. A visit with the church fathers is not a bad place to start.

David I. Smith is director of the Kuyers Institute for Christian Teaching and Learning and professor of education at Calvin University.

Acknowledgments

It has been a great joy to bring together within the pages of a single book my twin passions for church history and Christ-centered education. This work has been greatly enriched by the contributions of many others, to whom this acknowledgment is but a token of my gratitude for their assistance.

To my faculty reading group at Whitefield Academy, who faithfully gave up a portion of their Friday mornings to work through this manuscript, I am deeply indebted to each of you for your constructive criticism, ideas for further conversation partners and bibliographic references, and examples from your own classrooms that have helped illustrate the principles developed in this book. A special word of thanks, then, is due to Matthew David, Jesse Holthus, Jeff Horner, Kyle Justice, Katie Kling, David McBride, Christopher McDonald, Annalee Sellers, and Kevin Spingler. Other former and present colleagues who graciously provided feedback or shared examples utilized in this book include Tracy Blunier, Jessica Bonnem, Kevin Bracher, Erin Coleman, Hayley Davis, Trevor Moore, Nathan Stevens, and Jennifer Woods. My senior research assistants, Joel McKinney, Luke Sinclair, and Abbie Wickham, helped with the preparation of the manuscript.

Several correspondents have been gracious enough to read draft chapters and provide constructive feedback that has greatly enriched the quality of this book: Dan Beerens, D. Bruce Lockerbie, Aaron Schepps, and David I. Smith. As always, I owe a debt of gratitude to my own "soul friends" who have encouraged me throughout this journey: Greg Barnhill, R. J. Barthelmes, Bryan Klein, Dave McCune, Tony Melton, and Trevor Moore.

Michael Thomson, acquisitions editor at Cascade, was kind enough to attend a presentation I made on the relevance of John Chrysostom for modern Christian education at Calvin University in 2019 and proceeded to hound me, before I had even completed my previous book, to submit the proposal for the book now in your hands. His vision and passion for this project have served as an enormous encouragement to me throughout this process. The whole team at Cascade was just as fantastic to work with this second time around; special thanks to Rebecca Abbott, Blake Adams, George Callihan, Charlie Collier, Ian Creeger, Savanah N. Landerholm, and Matt Wimer.

Finally, I must acknowledge that the completion of this project was only possible thanks to my family's unceasing reservoirs of encouragement and support. My wife, Karisa, not only took on many extra hours of solo parenting but again served as my first line of feedback. Karisa, thank you for believing in this project and making so many sacrifices to help see it through to completion. To my children, Aliya, Asher, and Judah, I am glad to be able to devote more time again to building marble tracks, fighting Star Wars battles, and having gerbil adventures. And to my parents, Bob and Stephanie Hughes, thank you for your love and for providing the writing space, snacks, and coffee that fueled the writing of this book. This book is dedicated to my grandparents, Harold and Anne Hughes, whose legacy of faith I aspire to carry on to my own children and grandchildren.

Kyle Hughes
All Saints' Day, 2021

Timeline of Key Events and Texts

1

Introduction

Christian Education in a Convulsed Age

Christian schooling presents both profound challenges and incredible opportunities for those seeking to provide students with an education that contributes to their formation into disciples of Jesus Christ. While many teachers, professors, and administrators have discerned a call to this vocation precisely because of their desire to see young people grow into Christ's likeness, they may at times struggle to discern how best to carry out this work in an authentic and transformational way. We live in a convulsed age—as I write this, the United States is contending with far-reaching upheavals resulting from a global pandemic, economic downturn, and the legacy of racial inequality, and all of this in a broader time of intensifying political polarization, rapid technological and demographic change, and increasing environmental crisis. This is the world into which we are sending our students, young people who may already be experiencing the effects of these upheavals and uncertainties in their own lives, or perhaps are simply dealing with the more mundane (and yet, for them, no less real and significant) matters of meeting parental expectations, fitting in with peers, and facing learning difficulties. Likewise, many Christian educators are also experiencing convulsions in their work, adapting to new forms of virtual learning, staring down budget cuts, and wondering if their efforts are actually making any difference at all. As a teacher myself, I know that I often feel like I am just treading water. It can feel difficult enough to get through the required course content and grade yet another stack of essays; broader conversations about "the integration of faith and learning" can seem as distant and useless as the bottom of the sea.

And yet, the calling for Christian educators remains. Christ tells us that he came that we might have life—true, abundant, complete life—here and now, even in our present circumstances (John 10:10). It is this quality of life that we long for our students to taste and to see, as we have, that the Lord is good (Ps 34:8). It is a life in which we are reminded that we will have our portion of hardship and suffering, and yet it is in precisely those things that we will find true joy and communion with Christ (1 Pet 4:12–13). It is, moreover, a life in which we can become like trees planted by streams of water, yielding the fruit of love of God and love of neighbor for the healing of the world (Ps 1:3; Rev 22:2). This, then, is the life to which we endeavor to invite our students, even as we are very much in the process of figuring this out for ourselves. If anything, the present trials and tribulations of our world should only heighten the urgency with which we seek, for ourselves and for our students, the life that Christ brings. But how?

In light of the complexities and challenges of our present time and place, the early church fathers—those key figures of the first Christian centuries whose lives and writings guide the church's doctrine and practice to this day—would at first glance appear to be unlikely conversation partners for educators interested in making deeper connections between their Christian faith and the work of teaching and learning. It is my contention, however, that it is precisely in a time such as ours that the voices of our great forefathers need to be invited to the table. We need the church fathers to speak afresh that wisdom that has endured through the centuries and proven itself time and again to be a source of inspiration and edification for Christians through the ages. This book, then, is an attempt to advance a fresh vision of Christian teaching and learning by drawing upon the riches of the Christian tradition, synthesizing the wisdom of the church fathers with contemporary efforts to cultivate a distinctively Christian approach to education.

TWO KEY PRESUPPOSITIONS

Before beginning our engagement with the church fathers and what they can teach us about Christian education, a few words are in order to explain how I have arrived at my understanding of the purpose of Christian education and the relevance of the church fathers. While some readers may no doubt be eager to move on to begin engaging with the first of the church fathers we will examine in this book (and are welcome to do so), further attention to these two points will help make sense of the approach that undergirds the following chapters.

The Purpose of Christian Education

First, I hold that the goal of Christian education is not simply to produce graduates who *know* things about English, history, math, science, or even theology but rather to form graduates who *become* certain kinds of people—disciples of Jesus Christ. To validate this claim, we must briefly consider what we mean by "education" in the first place. In James K. A. Smith's influential definition, "An education . . . is a constellation of practices, rituals, and routines that inculcates a particular vision of the good life by inscribing or infusing that vision into the heart (the gut) by means of material, embodied practices."[1] For Christian educators, then, this means that "the primary goal of Christian education is the formation of a peculiar people—a people who desire the kingdom of God and thus undertake their vocations as an expression of that desire."[2] In other words, the ultimate end (that is, the *telos*) of Christian education is to help shape students' understanding of "the good life" as one that is centered on Christ and his kingdom, such that they are challenged to reorient more and more of their lives in light of the gospel. Rather than reducing students to what Smith provocatively calls "brains on a stick," empty containers into which the expert teacher pours her knowledge, this approach to education proceeds from a truly Christian anthropology that sees students, like all people, as embodied beings, who by means of their habits, relationships, and the Holy Spirit are formed into people who come to desire the things of God above the things of this world.[3]

1. J. Smith, *Desiring the Kingdom*, 26. The pursuit of "the good life," or *eudaimonia*, was in fact the central aim of ancient philosophy. Early Christians cast the gospel of Jesus Christ as the true *eudaimonia* or path to human flourishing. Besides being historically anchored, this language helps us see that Christian education must go beyond teaching a Christian worldview to forming an entire way of life, in which students pursue moral progress, cultivate virtue, and imitate Christ.

2. J. Smith, *Desiring the Kingdom*, 34; cf. Littlejohn and Evans, *Wisdom and Eloquence*, 18.

3. See further J. Smith, *Desiring the Kingdom*, 39–88. The epistemic foundations for such an approach are well articulated by Charles Taylor through his notion of the "social imaginary," for which see J. Smith, *Desiring the Kingdom*, 65–70. For a further popularization of this idea, see Warren, *Liturgy of the Ordinary*, 25–36. Likewise, Parker Palmer suggests that "where conventional education deals with abstract and impersonal facts and theories, an education shaped by Christian spirituality draws us toward incarnate and personal truth" (Palmer, *To Know as We Are Known*, 14).

We will return to this point below, but for now it will suffice to say that Smith helps us to see that the work of Christian education is in fact the work of discipleship, here carried out not in the sanctuary or on the mission field but in the classroom. By emphasizing the role of formational practices in building disciples, Smith points us to the realization that Christian education must include not just the selection of curriculum (the *what*) or the relationships being formed (the *who*) but even the process of teaching and learning itself (the *how*). This approach calls for the integration of faith and learning across all levels of the educational endeavor: in the curriculum and pedagogy, in the minds and lives of the teachers and students, and in the policies and ethos of the institution itself.[4] It involves, therefore, both an expansion of the imagination for rethinking some of these central aspects of the teaching task and a commitment to engaging in the formative practices and habits that will enable a Christian vision of the good life to take root in the deepest parts of a person's being.

Across his various works, but most clearly and recently in his book *On Christian Teaching*, David I. Smith has sought to unpack some elements of what such a distinctively Christian approach to education might include. What Smith correctly recognized was that most conversations about Christian teaching and learning were ignoring such formative classroom matters as the use of time and space, patterns of reflection and interaction, and types of homework and assessment.[5] As he insists, "An account of Christian education that focuses only on the truth of what is taught, and fails to address the meanings molded through *how* it is taught and learned is at best incomplete."[6] While conceding that "Christian faith cannot simply tell us how to teach or provide unique, copyrighted, Christian teaching moves," Smith still claims that "Christian faith can play a generative role in shaping pedagogy."[7] To unleash this process, he commends a model that involves examining how various aspects of the teaching and learning process might be viewed and practiced differently in light of the values and virtues of the kingdom of God.[8] A key initial element of Smith's proposal is the work of

4. See Littlejohn and Evans, *Wisdom and Eloquence*, 43; Gaebelein, *Pattern of God's Truth*. On some of the challenges related to the use of "faith-learning integration" language more generally, see Badley, "Clarifying 'Faith-Learning Integration'"; Glanzer, "Why We Should Discard." While acknowledging the limitations of this language, I continue to use it, given its wide acceptance in the literature. My notions of "faith" and "learning" will become apparent over the course of this book.

5. D. Smith, *On Christian Teaching*, 12.

6. D. Smith, *On Christian Teaching*, 4 (italics in original).

7. D. Smith, *On Christian Teaching*, 54.

8. D. Smith, *On Christian Teaching*, 69; simply put, the three steps of this model are to "see anew," "choose engagement," and "reshape practice."

expanding the imagination, casting a new vision of teaching and learning.[9] As Smith eloquently puts it: "Attending to faith's role within our pedagogical world involves being able to imagine afresh, to see anew, and for this we need not so much to think harder as to engage in the practices that nurture Christian imagination. We need to invest in becoming people capable of imagining in Christian ways, of seeing our classrooms through the lenses of grace, justice, beauty, delight, virtue, faith, hope, and love."[10] It is very much within this perspective on what it means to integrate faith and learning that I offer this book as a complement to Smith's provocative work.

The difficulty of this challenge should not be understated; there are, I believe, three major roadblocks to engaging with this task. The first is institutional. As others have recognized, the "prevailing view" in many Christian schools "assumes that Christian education more or less happens when Christians teach in Christian schools."[11] Indeed, it is easier for Christian educators to adopt the presuppositions, ideals, and values of the prevailing instrumentalist model of secular education, to add on a weekly chapel time and make some occasional efforts to connect Scripture to class content, than to do the work of moving in the direction of providing an education that would result in "the transformation of the school's educational goals, curriculum, pedagogy, student evaluation, and organizational structure."[12] What if this approach would make our school less appealing to colleges, graduate schools, or prospective employers? What if no one enrolled? There is a legitimate concern here for practical and economic realities that is understandable enough, and yet to the extent that we fail to embark upon this difficult work, our ability to provide a truly Christian education, and thereby participate in the work of forming Christian disciples and setting forth an authentic, countercultural Christian witness, suffers. While some institutional factors may lie outside of the control of many teachers, it is nevertheless the case that real organizational change is possible from the efforts of even small groups of teachers committed to advancing the cause of faith-learning integration in their classrooms.[13]

9. Again, "imagination" here and throughout is best understood in the context of Taylor's "social imaginary."

10. D. Smith, *On Christian Teaching*, 71.

11. Hull, "Aiming for Christian Education," 203.

12. Hull, "Aiming for Christian Education," 204. See also Dreher, *Benedict Option*, 147–50, 158–59.

13. See Palmer, *To Know as We Are Known*, 107–8: "Only in the heart searched and transformed by truth will new teaching techniques and strategies for institutional change find sure grounding. Only in such a heart will teachers find the courage to resist the conditions of academic life while we work and wait for institutional transformation."

The second roadblock is societal. As is widely recognized, America is now very much a post-Christian society, where Christianity no longer holds a religiously privileged position in the public square.[14] Indeed, the broader landscape of modern American spirituality appears to be tilting decisively away from orthodox expressions of Christianity.[15] As the philosopher Charles Taylor has demonstrated, we have entered a "secular age" in which we have moved "from a society in which it was virtually impossible not to believe in God, to one in which faith, even for the staunchest believer, is one human possibility among others."[16] Drawing on Taylor's work, Carl Trueman has identified a major cultural shift with profound repercussions for our society as the "prioritization of the individual's inner psychology—we might even say 'feelings' or 'intuitions'—for our sense of who we are and what the purpose of our lives is."[17] In such a context, the Christian appeal to the Bible and the traditional teachings of the church as in some sense authoritative is increasingly seen as problematic, if not outright dangerous. Still, there are signs of hope. As Gerald Sittser explains, while the decline of Christianity in the United States "has left the church concerned, confused, and sobered," it has also made the church more "curious and teachable, which is one reason why Christians are looking for new resources, movements, and models that might help us, as Christians living in the West, respond faithfully and winsomely to this new state of affairs."[18] As we will see below, it is my contention that the "new" approaches we need most are not so much those that are of recent origin but rather those that are being rediscovered after having been forgotten for a lengthy period of time and are now ready to speak afresh into our present circumstances.

The third roadblock is theological. The "triumph of the therapeutic" is seen not just in culture at large but even within much of the Christian church.[19] In their famous study of the religious beliefs of American teenagers, Christian Smith and Melinda Lundquist Denton identified "moralistic therapeutic deism" as the prevailing "religion" of many such young Americans. This belief system posits the existence of a deity who, from a safe distance from our affairs, just wants people to live good, moral lives

14. See further the fascinating portrayals of new "religious" movements in Burton, *Strange Rites.*

15. See Dreher, *Benedict Option,* 8–12.

16. Taylor, *Secular Age,* 3.

17. Trueman, *Rise and Triumph,* 23.

18. Sittser, *Resilient Faith,* 14.

19. For this phrase, see Trueman, *Rise and Triumph,* 301–37.

so that they can be happy and fulfilled.[20] For Smith and Denton, this was not so much a conscious theological development as it was a reflection of a broader American social context of "therapeutic individualism" emphasizing subjective personal experience and self-fulfillment.[21] In any event, while this kind of thinking is certainly not characteristic of all American teenagers today, nor is it limited to younger generations exclusively, moralistic therapeutic deism is nevertheless the form of "Christianity" that informs much of our present teaching context. The challenge, then, is to help our students—and, indeed, ourselves—enter into a more meaningful and more orthodox understanding of what it means to be a Christian, one in which we are striving to submit the entirety of our lives to Christ as his disciples, such that we "interpret and live all of life within the Biblical drama of creation, fall, redemption, and restoration."[22] Rather than moralistic therapeutic deism, we are called to a faith characterized by what the German theologian and martyr Dietrich Bonhoeffer described as a "single-minded obedience" in which we follow Jesus on the road of self-denial and suffering, which is "the badge of true discipleship" and the means by which we share in Christ's own life.[23] This, then, is what we mean by discipleship: the daily work of training our affections away from the things of this world such that, by the power of the Holy Spirit, we are transformed into Christ's likeness in every aspect of our lives. As we put off the old, we put on the new (Eph 4:22–24), learning to find and embrace the presence of God in every aspect of our daily living.[24]

We will unpack in more detail the exact nature of this understanding of the Christian life and how to go about walking alongside of our students on this journey in the chapters that follow. For now, though, it will suffice to note that this book proceeds from the belief that the goal of Christian education is nothing less than the formation of disciples of Jesus Christ, an aim which requires a thoughtful and comprehensive approach to the integration of faith and learning that impacts every aspect of the educational endeavor. Thankfully, given the enormous challenge of this task, we have a powerful and yet underappreciated resource to help us in developing such an approach: the church fathers.

20. C. Smith and Denton, *Soul Searching*, 162–65.

21. C. Smith and Denton, *Soul Searching*, 172–75.

22. Glanzer, "Why We Should Discard," 43.

23. Bonhoeffer, *Cost of Discipleship*, 79; cf. Mark 8:35–36.

24. See further the classic work of Brother Lawrence, *Practice of Presence of God*; on discipleship more broadly, see Willard, *Renovation of the Heart*, 63–75.

The Relevance of the Church Fathers

The second main assumption of this book is that the close study of the teachings of the church fathers can provide a new lens for thinking about Christian teaching and learning. Considering the above section, we might rightly ask what it would look like to go about actually nurturing a Christian imagination that has the potential to transform the way we see Christian teaching and learning. We might wonder, too, what habits we could engage in, as individuals or with other teachers or even with our students, that would deepen the role of faith in our classrooms. There are, of course, the basic disciplines of the Christian life: reading the Bible, prayer, and corporate worship. We can exchange ideas with our colleagues and attend conferences. But most Christian educators are not trained biblical scholars or theologians, instinctively able to bridge the pages of the New Testament or the liturgy of the church's worship to the work of the science classroom or the computer lab. Likewise, many churches have dropped the ball on faith formation for their own people, complicating our efforts to reach our students when we feel so inadequate in our own spiritual lives. For these reasons, we need expert guides who can help show us the way. David Smith himself recognizes this need: "The cultivation of a Christian imagination, one rooted in both Scriptures and a communion of saints that stretches beyond the bounds of our own social and historical context, can help us to see our tasks and contexts anew. Throughout Christian history, there have been thinkers who have allowed their vision of pedagogy to be framed and shaped by the imagery of Scripture and the practices of the church, and they can help us to imagine differently."[25] Indeed, getting outside of our own time and place can, like a semester abroad, shake loose some of our certainties about the way things must be. In this way, the history of the church, and the lives of those saints who have gone before us, can indeed provide opportunities for expanding our imaginations.

Are the early church fathers, though, really adequate guides for this particular journey? Within some evangelical Protestant circles of Christian education, there is often a bias towards an understanding of church history that sees the Protestant Reformation as the retrieval of "true New Testament Christianity," as if everything between the New Testament and the Reformation had been a giant mistake. Often there is simply an ignorance of church history altogether. There are, however, many hopeful signs that

---

25. D. Smith, *On Christian Teaching*, 93. At this point in his book, Smith briefly gestures to the preaching of Bernard of Clairvaux as an illustrative example of this point before referring readers to his *Teaching and Christian Imagination*, which engages with other late medieval and Reformation-era Christian thought.

the evangelical church is increasingly recognizing, as the great Protestant reformers themselves had acknowledged, the significance of the great tradition for the present and future of the Christian faith. This is seen, for instance, in an increased interest among evangelical scholars in the early church, as there is a growing awareness that the spirituality and theology of the early church can provide a solid grounding for the faith in the ever-shifting sands of the present day.[26] Likewise, the burgeoning movement of a large number of younger evangelicals into more historic and liturgical expressions of the Christian faith suggests that this book's approach is tapping into a broader movement in which the Spirit is calling us back to rediscover the fullness of our heritage as Christians.[27]

Thus, this book posits that the church fathers represent a significant and largely untapped resource in expanding our imaginations for thinking about Christian teaching and learning. Despite having lived in what can seem like an entirely foreign world to us today, the early church fathers, like us, sought to explain, live out, and pass on the Christian faith in the midst of a complex and ever-changing world, characterized by pluralism, syncretism, and materialism, grappling with the fallout from plagues, economic upheavals, and the mass migrations of peoples. In so doing they left us with a variety of ideas, metaphors, and practices that constitute something of a "spiritual treasure box" from which we can draw. The church has long taught that the lives of these ancient church fathers were characterized by orthodoxy of doctrine, holiness of life, and approval from other Christians.[28] Not only have many of their ideas stood the test of time, but the church fathers themselves were (and still are) considered worthy of emulation. If nothing else, the example of those heroes of the faith who came before us can inspire and encourage us in our own vocations, reminding us that we are part of a grand story that transcends our own lives.[29] We are, the Apostles' Creed reminds us, part of a great "communion of saints," connecting us, in Christ, to other believers across time and space. Lest we succumb to the arrogance of historical amnesia or the pride of presentism, we must allow others, even

26. See D. Williams, *Evangelicals and Tradition*; Ortlund, *Theological Retrieval for Evangelicals*. The Protestant Reformers were, of course, themselves motivated by their study of the church fathers to recover the spirituality and theology of the early church, suggesting that current Protestant amnesia regarding church history was not in line with their original ideals.

27. While evidence for this phenomenon remains largely anecdotal, some early analysis of this movement is found in Bevins, *Ever Ancient, Ever New*. On the importance of reappropriating this heritage in our present times, see Dreher, *Benedict Option*, 100–121.

28. Litfin, *Getting to Know*, 19; cf. Heb 12:1.

29. See Litfin, *Getting to Know*, 29.

(and perhaps especially!) those from radically different circumstances, to speak into our own situation, and the church fathers are the most time-honored place from which to start. If nothing else, our study of our Christian predecessors can help us to challenge the mistakes and point out the blind spots of Christian thinking in our present context.

This book focuses on one specific aspect of the heritage of the early church as it pertains to Christian teaching and learning: *ascetical theology* as the means of forming disciples of Christ. As traditionally understood, classical asceticism (from the Greek *askēsis*) refers to the practices of self-discipline and self-denial by which one seeks to advance along a given philosophical or religious path. To modern Christians, such a description may conjure up images of early Christian ascetics living on pillars in the desert or cloistered monks whipping their backs in penance for their sins. However, I have in view a more expansive notion of what we might term an "ascetical spirituality." While we will indeed wish to avoid some of the extremes of early Christian asceticism, it is nevertheless the case that our baptismal vows push us to embrace elements of the ascetical life.[30] In the Anglican tradition, for instance, the *Book of Common Prayer* directs the baptismal candidate (or sponsors) to "renounce the empty promises and deadly deceits of this world that corrupt and destroy the creatures of God," and to "renounce the sinful desires of the flesh that draw you from the love of God."[31] Thus, Greg Peters writes, "Asceticism, that most monastic of practices, is expected of all Christian believers by virtue of our baptism and is characterized by balance and moderation."[32] In an age where comfort and consumption are privileged above all else, the ascetical tradition calls us back to a way of life in which our desires are rightly ordered.

In this book, then, I follow Martin Thornton's description of ascetical theology as that which is "dealing with the fundamental duties and disciplines of the Christian life, which nurture the ordinary ways of prayer, and which discover and foster those spiritual gifts and graces constantly found in ordinary people."[33] In other words, ascetical theology focuses on those practices and virtues by which, in cooperation with the Holy Spirit, we progress in the spiritual life. These practices and virtues must not, however, become an end unto themselves; rather, they are the means by which we

---

30. See Peters, *Monkhood of All Believers*, 142–43.

31. Anglican Church, *Book of Common Prayer*, 164.

32. Peters, *Monkhood of All Believers*, 142. This theme is found in the New Testament itself; see, for instance, Christ's forty days of fasting and prayer in the wilderness (Matt 4:1–2 pars.) or Paul's language of disciplining his body (1 Cor 9:27).

33. Thornton, *English Spirituality*, 19.

journey towards our ultimate purpose or *telos*.[34] Historically, this *telos* has been identified not as "going to heaven," but rather as attaining the beatific vision, or, to use other words, the contemplation of God (Ps 27:4, 8).[35] This deeply biblical idea is perhaps best exemplified by Paul's words that "we all, with unveiled face, beholding the glory of the Lord, are being transformed into the same image from one degree of glory to another" (2 Cor 3:18); thus, in turning away from ourselves and seeking the face of God (Ps 105:4), we find that we are actually becoming more like Christ. As articulated by the church fathers, contemplation is "a foretaste in the present life of the vision of God that characterizes the life to come."[36] At the heart of this contemplation is a personal experience of God; through ascetical practices such as prayer, fasting, and the devotional reading of Scripture, we are, by the power of the Holy Spirit, transformed into the image of Christ. We will perhaps even, like Paul, find our hearts drawn ever nearer to God's presence in a profound encounter with divine love (2 Cor 12:1–10). To this end, we are called to develop in ourselves and in our students what James K. A. Smith calls the "habits of *daily* worship," engaging students in those common practices that redirect the heart to God.[37] It is, therefore, a primary contention of this book that the invitation to ascetical practices and virtues is a neglected and yet powerful means of forming our students in the Christian way into the kinds of people who do not just know about God but will become what Hans Boersma calls "apprentices" of God, by which Boersma indicates those who are guided by God in Christ "along the process of salvation" such that they are increasingly habituated to God's presence and able to grow in their capacity to behold God in Christ.[38]

Therefore, the truth to which the church fathers ultimately point us is that the spirit—that is, the defining or typical element—of Christian teaching is one in which the Spirit—that is, God's own empowering presence—infuses all aspects of our work. If the goal of Christian education, and

---

34. See Peters, *Monkhood of All Believers*, 93: "Asceticism, as an essential component of spiritual growth, is the voluntary abstention from food and drink, sleep, wealth, sexual activity, and so on (for a period of time or permanently), for the purpose of maintaining inner attentiveness to God and achieving union with God."

35. See Thornton, *English Spirituality*, 20–23. For a comprehensive treatment of this theme throughout the Christian tradition, see Boersma, *Seeing God*.

36. Peters, *Monkhood of All Believers*, 34. See also the definition of Thornton, *English Spirituality*, 20: "a direct, if dim perception of God as distinct from the discursive, imaginative, and intellectual processes of 'meditation,' vocal prayer, and liturgical worship."

37. J. Smith, *Desiring the Kingdom*, 211 (italics in original). On the connection between asceticism and liturgy, see further Peters, *Monkhood of All Believers*, 103–10.

38. Boersma, *Seeing God*, 388–89.

indeed the Christian life in general, is to be formed into Christ's likeness, to become disciples of Christ, we can take heart from the knowledge that this is the work of the very Spirit of God, who seeks to draw our students into relationship with himself, not simply for their own salvation but for his purposes of mission and renewal in the world. Thus, even in this convulsed age, even with the enormity of the task before us, we have access to "power from on high" (Luke 24:49), to the Spirit who can give us the gifts we need to carry out our vocation (1 Cor 12:4–7) and can produce in us and in our students the fruit that characterizes a Spirit-empowered life (Gal 5:22–23).[39] Undergirding all of the patristic claims we will examine in this book is the understanding that the Spirit leads believers into all truth (John 16:13), a truth that the church fathers believed would be received not just intellectually but in a way that is "inescapably participatory and transformative."[40] In other words, transformation happens not so much when we encounter ideas about God as when we encounter God himself; by the Spirit, God makes us a new creation, gives us new birth, and puts a new heart within us as we become increasingly transformed into the image of Christ.[41] Thus, over the following chapters of this book, we will see how the church fathers present us with a historically rooted and theologically rich means of nurturing our imaginations as we seek, by the power of the Holy Spirit, to cultivate a distinctively Christian pedagogy adequate for the task before us.

AN INVITATION TO THE JOURNEY

Many of the ideas we will encounter in this book will no doubt at first glance seem quite foreign or even strange, especially for those who have not spent much time in the company of the church fathers. My encouragement, then, is simply to consider this book as an invitation to a journey of reflecting on all that we do as Christian educators. We need not adopt wholesale every aspect of the church fathers' thinking in order to find ourselves challenged to reimagine aspects of our classrooms. As your guide on this journey, I write as someone who has not myself "arrived" but has perhaps a unique vantage point for undertaking this endeavor: my formal training is in the history and literature of early Christianity, not education. And while I have taught at both the university and high school levels, I am also, as an ordained Anglican minister, deeply invested in the work of education within the context

---

39. See further Keener, *Gift and Giver*, 74–82.

40. Hughes, *How the Spirit Became God*, 136.

41. See Ezek 36:26–27; John 3:5–6; 2 Cor 3:18; 5:17; Eph 4:17–24; Col 3:9–10; see further Keener, *Gift and Giver*, 72–74.

of the local church. As a result, I hope that a broad array of Christian educators in a wide range of contexts will consider taking this journey with me.

To chart our journey ahead, we will draw on the insights of the church fathers to explore five key questions at the heart of teaching and learning. *Who are we as teachers? Who are our students? What are we teaching? How are we teaching? How do we plan for growth?* The basic structure of each of the following chapters of the book is to answer one of these questions by drawing upon the insights of a selected church father whose writings have the potential to stimulate our ability to reimagine this aspect of Christian education and to consider what kinds of habits and practices can help bring this new vision to life. Each chapter begins with a brief introduction to the life of the relevant church father so that readers unfamiliar with these giants of the faith can have a sense of the context in which the church fathers wrote. The subject matter of each chapter is largely discrete, and yet a distinct, coherent vision of Christian education gradually takes shape as each chapter builds upon earlier ones.

Thus, for those who, like me, need all the help they can get in being Christian educators in this convulsed age, I offer the following reflections not so much as "a new teaching with authority" (Mark 1:27) but rather as an invitation to consider with me, a fellow pilgrim on this journey, new ways in which we can consider how the teachings of the one to whom "all authority in heaven and on earth has been given" (Matt 28:18) might apply to our work as Christian educators in these troubled times. We will begin, therefore, by seeking to shed light on the most basic of questions: *what does it mean to be a Christian teacher?*

Ch. 1 Overview
    2 main ideas
  · Education is meant to make disciples
    of Christ
  · Education should include a study
    of our Christian forefathers / heritage /
                                history

2

Who Are We as Teachers?

Gregory the Great and Contemplative Spirituality

As we set out on this journey, taking along the church fathers as our companions for the task of reimagining the nature of Christian teaching and learning, we begin by focusing on teachers themselves. While the world and contemporary literature on Christian education supply us with many ways of conceiving what it means to be a teacher, in this chapter we will focus on a single, perhaps surprising aspect of a teacher's identity: the teacher as a spiritual director helping to disciple and guide his or her students. Surprisingly, given the centrality of this aspect of the teaching profession in motivating many Christian educators to pursue their line of work, there has not been adequate attention to how the Christian tradition's understanding of pastoral theology and spiritual direction can translate into the classroom.[1] Indeed, while conceptions of what it means to be a teacher have varied considerably over the centuries and from culture to culture, the Christian tradition historically has steadfastly refused to separate the work of education from that of discipleship. To help us think through this dynamic and

---

1. For one significant exception, see the excellent discussion of the spiritual formation of teachers in Palmer, *To Know as We Are Known*, 106–25. While Palmer draws primarily on the desert fathers for his discussions, his conclusions regarding the need for silence and solitude echo my own. By comparison, for a more typical approach, simply emphasizing the significance of a Christian teacher's worldview more generally, see Gaebelein, *Pattern of God's Truth*, 35–53.

its implications in more detail, we will turn to Gregory the Great's landmark *Book of Pastoral Rule*.

Gregory the Great (ca. 540–604) lived in a time of cataclysmic convulsions. In the decades following the fall of the Western Roman Empire in 476, conditions in the city of Rome deteriorated. Warfare resulting from the continued migration of Germanic tribes into the Italian peninsula led to widespread devastation, famine, and instability, while flooding and recurring outbreaks of plague further accelerated depopulation and societal decay.[2] In the words of historian Peter Brown, by the end of the sixth century, "Rome was a ghost of its former self."[3] Following the collapse of centralized administration and the removal of Byzantine protection, dramatically symbolized by the city's people tearing down many of its grand monuments and edifices to shore up its failing walls, political authority in the city of Rome increasingly fell into the hands of the bishop of Rome—the pope.[4]

The spiritual condition of the Roman people in this time was not much better. Following the conversion of the emperor Constantine and the end of persecution in the early fourth century, new converts from the upper ranks of society joined the church in large numbers, bringing with them wealth and power that would have lasting, negative significance for the future of Christianity. One of the many results of this transformation was the growth of monasticism, as Christians seeking what they perceived to be a deeper and more authentic level of discipleship left behind traditional society to pursue holiness and moral perfection in the wilderness, first as individuals and then, increasingly, in communities. Renouncing the trappings of wealth and status, these monks committed themselves to a life of asceticism, which focuses on limiting or renouncing worldly pleasures in order to pursue the path of spiritual growth; special attention was devoted to those contemplative practices of prayer and engagement with Scripture that were perceived as means of increasing intimacy and unity with God.[5]

Into this context stepped the man whom history would remember as Pope Gregory I, or simply Gregory the Great, who stood at the nexus of these two developments. Before ascending to the papacy, Gregory had served as

2. See further Markus, *Gregory the Great*, 3–8; more generally, see Brown, *Rise of Western Christendom*, 190–215.

3. Brown, *Rise of Western Christendom*, 190.

4. See González, *Story of Christianity*, 1:285.

5. See Demacopoulos, *Gregory the Great*, 19. On the development of asceticism and its inroads into the church hierarchy during the post-Nicene period, see Rapp, *Holy Bishops in Late Antiquity*, 100–152; Brown, *Rise of Western Christendom*, 81–84, 111–13. Benedict of Nursia, significant both as an exemplar of this movement and as a major influence on Gregory, will be the subject of ch. 5 of this book.

prefect of the city of Rome, which provided him with invaluable administrative experience that would shape his leadership of the church. Gregory then left this post in order to pursue the monastic life, wherein he would embrace a strong strain of asceticism that would also greatly influence his papacy. Ultimately, however, his time at his monastic retreat was cut short by the demands of the current pope, Pelagius II, who sent him as an emissary to the Byzantine emperor in Constantinople. This set in motion a series of events that would culminate in Gregory's own election to the papal seat in 590, where he would nevertheless continue to promote an ascetical, contemplative spirituality.[6] Gregory's personal spiritual journey uniquely shaped his papacy insofar as he aimed at synthesizing the active life of public ministry and the contemplative life of the monastery in what we might call the "active contemplative life."[7] Gregory's preparation for the papacy positioned him well to address Rome's administrative and spiritual problems, and in so doing set the course for much of medieval church history.

At the beginning of his papacy, Gregory wrote his *Book of Pastoral Rule*, which in many ways represents his synthesis of the active and the contemplative as applied to the work of pastoral leadership. This book would, in fact, "become the most widely circulating and influential treatise on spiritual direction in Christian history."[8] What is particularly intriguing for our purposes is that the *Pastoral Rule* was meant for a broad audience; Gregory seems to be writing not just to bishops or priests but to monastic leaders as well, thereby encompassing nearly everyone who in his day held responsibilities involving the spiritual care of others. Many of these leaders indeed had significant educational components to their vocation.[9] We will, therefore, speak of Gregory as writing to "spiritual leaders" in a general sense, one which in our time would surely include Christian educators, who share in the responsibilities of encouraging students' spiritual growth. That is to say, while very few Christian educators may be ordained clergy or have taken monastic vows, Gregory's pastoral theology is relevant to the extent that the work of Christian education requires going beyond simply the dissemination of information or even promoting certain values or leadership skills to engaging with the profound task of shepherding students' souls. Of course, we live in a world very different from Gregory's; in particular,

6. For further overview of the life of Gregory, see Deanesly, *History of Medieval Church*, 15–28; Markus, *Gregory the Great*, 8–14; Demacopoulos, *Gregory the Great*, 1–4.

7. Demacopoulos, *Gregory the Great*, 59.

8. Demacopoulos, *Gregory the Great*, 53.

9. Demacopoulos, *Gregory the Great*, 55; on the audience of this work, see further Raab, "Gregory, Marmion," 27–28.

Gregory's intense theology of asceticism, which undergirds his *Pastoral Rule* at every turn, presents a model of the Christian life that feels foreign, and undoubtedly unattainable (and perhaps even undesirable), to many of us today.[10] Still, this chapter will demonstrate the continued relevance of Gregory's ideas for our present context.

As we seek to understand and apply Gregory's pastoral insights for our contemporary work of Christian education, we will look first at the essential qualifications and qualities of a person entrusted with the care of souls and then examine how the concept of spiritual direction provides a concrete access point for carrying out the work of spiritual formation in the classroom. Warning: the path that Gregory will suggest is difficult and demanding. We will likely be tempted to feel that what Gregory is proposing is impossible, especially insofar as many of us may not have engaged with much theology or approaches to spiritual direction as part of our teacher training. Nevertheless, I believe that even our humblest efforts at walking these ancient paths will lead us to living waters (John 7:37–39).

QUALIFICATIONS FOR SPIRITUAL LEADERS

Gregory opens the first book of his *Pastoral Rule* with the following summary statement: "No one presumes to teach an art that he has not first mastered through study. How foolish it is therefore for the inexperienced to assume pastoral authority when the care of souls is the art of arts" (*PR*, 1.1).[11] Gregory then proceeds to unpack this claim in light of his own context; as he perceived it, the wrong types of people, driven by the wrong sorts of motives or displaying the wrong kinds of behaviors, were occupying positions of spiritual leadership, thus failing to be the kind of active contemplative role models envisioned by Gregory. As we will see, Gregory can challenge us as Christian educators to better reflect on our own motives for teaching and how we actually behave as teachers.

Right Motives

Gregory first identifies a group of spiritual leaders who have sought their positions because of their own greed and vanity. With particular relevance for Christian educators, Gregory alerts us to the fact that some people pursue

10. On Gregory's ascetical theology, see further Demacopoulos, *Gregory the Great*, 17–30.

11. All quotations from Gregory's *Book of Pastoral Rule* are taken from the translation of Demacopoulos.

positions of spiritual leadership in order to boost their own ego, for they "want to be seen as teachers and they lust to be superior to others" (*PR*, 1.1). As for greed, while presumably very few teachers today have pursued their vocation out of a desire for riches, those who are underpaid might allow this to fester resentment and anger towards their work. Likewise, concerning vanity, the reality is that the teacher-student relationship intrinsically creates a power structure that is appealing to those who need affirmation or are "nourished by the thought of subordinating others" (*PR*, 1.8). For some of us, the classroom is the one place where we can be an unmatched and unchallenged authority figure. While we may not get these things from our peers or our own families, we can, to satisfy the needs of our pride, require obedience and respect from our students at the expense of actual teaching and learning.[12] There is, of course, something healthy in students learning to submit to authority, and yet there is a temptation for us to find our identity and status in the ways that our students follow our dictates and seek to please us (at least insofar as it nets them a strong recommendation letter). Given the formative nature of the teacher-student relationship, the sinful motivations and attitudes that inhabit our own understanding of our vocation may very well be transmitted to our students. As Gregory summarizes, quoting the words of Christ, "If the blind lead the blind, then both fall into the pit" (*PR*, 1.1; cf. Matt 15:14). The first task that Gregory calls us to, then, is to consider our motivations for becoming teachers and spiritual leaders and, where necessary, repent of those impure motivations that threaten to sabotage our teaching ministries.[13]

Right Behaviors

Gregory then turns to consider a second group of spiritual leaders whose teaching he considers ineffectual: "Moreover, there are some who investigate spiritual precepts with great care but trample upon what they analyze by the way in which they live" (*PR*, 1.2). While it may be tempting to put this solely on teachers of Bible or theology, the reality of working at a Christian school or publicly identifying as a Christian means that no Christian educator is immune from this challenge. Young people, we all know, are uniquely

12. Palmer, *To Know as We Are Known*, 109: "The teacher who lacks humility will be unable to create a space for any voice except his or her own."

13. See further Purves, *Pastoral Theology*, 63–64. This question of motivations is an important, albeit in my experience largely lacking, element of the interview process for teaching positions. It would also be worth exploring with veteran teachers how their motivations for teaching may have evolved over time.

gifted at sniffing out hypocrisy by identifying those gaps between what we practice and what we preach. It does not take much to break trust and lose credibility with students, something that threatens to affect not only the students' view of us but their attitude towards the Christian faith more generally. Not for nothing, then, does Gregory issue a sharp condemnation of such teachers, quoting the Lord's saying, "He that scandalizes one of these little ones who believes in me, it would be better for him that a millstone was hung around his neck and that he was cast into the depth of the sea" (*PR*, 1.2; cf. Matt 18:6). Gregory thus challenges Christian educators with a second test, forcing us to consider if our words and our actions line up and, as needed, repent of those ways in which we have brought disrepute on ourselves and the gospel.[14]

Gregory wants us to feel the weight of our spiritual responsibilities, what he calls "the burden of leadership" (*PR*, 1.3). He does this precisely because he is aware of how difficult it is to be a spiritual leader in the context of the active (as opposed to contemplative) life. Gregory understands that, unlike the life of a cloistered monk, active ministry in the world pulls our attention in myriad directions and draws us away from opportunities to reflect critically on our motivations and actions. Our natural tendency, Gregory suggests, is to fall into a state wherein "the mind is such a stranger to self-examination that it does not consider the damage that it suffers and is ignorant of the extent to which it errs" (*PR*, 1.4). Indeed, the busy workday of a teacher makes it very difficult to find the time and space necessary to develop an inner life that could sustain a teaching career steeped in virtue. In particular, the tyranny of deadlines—to turn around essays with quality feedback for growth, to finish a lesson plan for the class that starts in just a few minutes, to rush across campus to be on time for that next meeting— conspires to keep educators from crucial periods of self-reflection.

In Gregory's time, concerns of this nature led some, including Gregory himself, to fear taking on positions of spiritual leadership that might undermine their lives of holiness. Some contemplatives would thereby refuse to accept such positions, even to the point of resisting God's call (*PR*, 1.5). Gregory pushes back against this group as well: "When these men contemplate their own spiritual advantages and do not consider anyone else, they lose these goods because they desire to keep them for themselves" (*PR*, 1.5). Therefore, he writes, it is fine for these contemplatives to declare themselves unworthy of taking on spiritual leadership, provided that this humility is subordinated to an obedience that will heed God's call to the active life, if it comes (*PR*, 1.6). I suspect that few, if any, educators in our context would

14. See further Purves, *Pastoral Theology*, 64–65.

identify with this group of rigorous contemplatives, and that it is rather the other group, which desires leadership and authority too much, that is most relevant. In emphasizing how the contemplatives of his day, as well as the prophets of old, rightly understood the heavy burden of leadership, Gregory amplifies his criticism of those who "because of their selfish appetites" have no hesitations in taking on positions of spiritual leadership (*PR*, 1.7).[15] Even if, therefore, we sense a call to the teaching vocation, we would be wise to approach it with a kind of holy awe at the task before us.

In sum, Gregory compares such unqualified teachers who purport to be physicians of the soul to doctors who know nothing about medicine (*PR*, 1.1) or who are themselves grievously ill (*PR*, 1.9). The positive qualifications for spiritual leadership, then, are the opposite of these things: spiritual leaders themselves must have been schooled in the ways of God and have so progressed in their sanctification that they can genuinely be held up as models for all to emulate. Gregory summarizes some of his qualifications for spiritual leadership as follows: "He must, therefore, be the model for everyone. He must be devoted entirely to the example of good living. He must be dead to the passions of the flesh and live a spiritual life. He must have no regard for worldly prosperity and never cower in the face of adversity" (*PR*, 1.10). And this is just the beginning of Gregory's list!

As we read this and Gregory's further list of qualifications, we no doubt feel quite uncomfortable and intimidated. Perhaps we fear that Gregory would look at us and see nothing more than failures and frauds. Even as we recognize the many differences between Gregory's time and our own, I think it is important that we sit with this feeling for a bit, to feel the weight of our responsibilities in shaping the souls of our students. Not for nothing did James warn us, "Not many of you should become teachers, my brothers, for you know that those of you who teach will be judged with greater strictness" (Jas 3:1; cf. *PR*, 1.3). What Gregory ultimately wants us to see is that it is the example of our character that teaches as much as anything else we do. In this book on teaching and learning, then, it is only fitting that we start with the character of the teacher and recognize the enormous impact that the teacher's own life has on the quality of his or her Christian witness.[16]

While we may not ever meet Gregory's lofty standards for spiritual leadership in his context, the fact is that (like it or not!) we are already in

15. On Gregory's understanding of proper humility in the context of the monastic tradition, see Raab, "Gregory, Marmion," 29–30.

16. Raab, "Gregory, Marmion," 29: "Gregory is utterly concerned with the personal qualities of spiritual directors. Indeed, he prioritizes these personal qualities and will only proceed to discuss ministerial method after laying the foundation for ministry in the character of the minister."

positions of profound spiritual authority on account of our vocation as Christian teachers. Rather than shrink from Gregory's challenge, ignoring what he has to say or quitting our jobs in despair, we have an opportunity to lean into this vision of teaching from a place of pure motives and a life that is in conformity with what we profess to believe. The first step in doing this is to take seriously Gregory's aforementioned worry that, among busy Christians such as ourselves, "the mind is such a stranger to self-examination that it does not consider the damage that it suffers and is ignorant of the extent to which it errs" (PR, 1.4). In other words, Gregory suggests that we must examine, align, and balance our interior (spiritual) and exterior (physical) lives. This process can proceed only from the messy and uncomfortable process of self-examination.

The work of a teacher, like that of other helping professions, presents a wealth of emotionally charged moments that threaten to inflame unhealed wounds. By tending to our own spiritual and emotional health, we will be better able to deal with inevitable things like conflict and tension both inside and outside the classroom, gradually becoming transformed into the kinds of people that we would want our students to emulate.[17] Before getting into specific practices that can help move us in this direction, as we will explore in the next section of this chapter, we may for now simply note that growing in our own self-awareness first necessitates cultivating spaces where we can listen to our emotions, hopes, and fears, and bring them before the presence of God. It is, in fact, those of us engaging in active ministries in the world, living busy lives, who are perhaps most in need of the classic contemplative spiritual disciplines of silence and solitude.[18] What if, then, what we need most to become better teachers is not another workshop or another degree but a conscious decision to make space to cultivate our own life with God? What if the best thing we could do for our students is to invest in our own spiritual lives, to become the kinds of spiritually and emotionally healthy people who can give to our students from the overflow of our own intimacy with Christ?[19] In so doing, we may just find that our motives and our actions are increasingly being brought into conformity with the gospel that we want to point our students to each day in our classroom.

17. See further Scazzero, *Emotionally Healthy Spirituality*, 117–37; Willard, *Renovation of the Heart*, 63–232. On self-examination as a foundational practice of Christian spirituality, see Peters, *Monkhood of All Believers*, 144–49.

18. See Scazzero, *Emotionally Healthy Spirituality*, 63. On silence and solitude as spiritual disciplines, see further Foster, *Celebration of Discipline*, 96–109; Palmer, *To Know as We Are Known*, 117–24. This was, of course, Christ's own pattern during his earthly ministry.

19. See D. Smith and Felch, *Teaching and Christian Imagination*, 60–65.

QUALITIES OF A SPIRITUAL LEADER

Having set out his qualifications for spiritual leadership, Gregory next considers the qualities that should characterize the life of a spiritual leader. In opening book 2 of his *Pastoral Rule*, Gregory asserts, "The active life of the leader ought to transcend that of the people in proportion to how the life of a shepherd outshines that of his flock" (*PR*, 2.1). Indeed, we thus discover right at the outset of this section that Gregory will continue to refuse watering down or compromising his standards, given the high stakes of the work of Christian ministry. Ever practical, Gregory proceeds to offer a set of concrete qualities that collectively aim to pull together elements of contemplative spirituality for the active life. By continuing to emphasize his notion of active contemplation, Gregory not only echoes and extends his qualifications for spiritual leadership but also provides a consistent thread that holds together all of the qualities that he goes on to elaborate.[20]

Purity of Thought

First, Gregory calls us to *purity of thought* (*PR*, 2.2). As we saw above, Gregory is deeply concerned about the motivations and behaviors of spiritual leaders, lest our sinful tendencies or hypocrisy adversely affect those who look up to us. The best way to protect ourselves from these things, Gregory insists, is a cleansed mind that avoids the pollutions of the world. To this end, Gregory encourages following the guidance of reason, meditating on the lives of the saints, and discerning between good and evil.[21] As teachers, and therefore spiritual leaders in our classrooms, we must carefully guard the "inputs" into our lives, for they will in large part determine the "outputs" that will bleed over into our witness. Not for nothing did Paul instruct us "whatever is true, whatever is honorable, whatever is just, whatever is pure, whatever is lovely, whatever is commendable, if there is any excellence, if there is anything worthy of praise, think about these things" (Phil 4:8). Practically speaking, for instance, this means that the music, media, and entertainment we consume should look different from that of a typical student or our non-Christian friends and neighbors. This is true not just with respect

20. See further Evans, *Thought of Gregory the Great*, 23; Purves, *Pastoral Theology*, 69–73.

21. Over the course of *PR*, 2.2–4, Gregory develops his argument on the basis of a beautiful allegorical interpretation of the Old Testament priestly garments in Exod 28. While the minutiae of his exegesis is beyond the scope of our analysis, interested readers should consult a translation of these sections for a good example of how Gregory read and applied Scripture.

to the quality of such content but the quantity of our engagement with it as well. For instance, to the extent that endlessly scrolling through our social media feeds builds in us an appetite for mindlessness and short-circuits the brain's capacity for maintaining focus in general, even our engagement with neutral or positive inputs can, based on the formative properties of the medium, shape our lives and our witness. While there is something to be said for being culturally aware and engaged, deliberately choosing to feast on those things that point us to the fullness of Christ reshapes our appetites and fills our spiritual bellies.

Example for Others

Second, we are to *set an example for others through our actions*. After all, Gregory reminds us, "the one who is compelled by his position to speak of the highest things is also compelled, by necessity, to show the highest things by his example" (*PR*, 2.3). Recalling his concern for alignment between what we say and what we do, Gregory continues to emphasize that it is our actions, in combination with our words, that make far more of an impact on others than do our words by themselves. Gregory again identifies the spiritual leader's interior life as the basis for an exterior life of virtue, arguing that the internal, contemplative love of God is inseparable from the external, active love of neighbor. As teachers, we certainly always want to be mindful of not doing good deeds in order to impress our peers and students (Matt 6:1–4), and yet, as the Lord commands us, "let your light shine before others, so that they may see your good works and give glory to your Father who is in heaven" (Matt 5:16). Perhaps, then, Gregory is simply calling us towards those moment-by-moment, small acts of kindness, justice, and mercy that we extend towards our students, colleagues, and parents that, over time, begin to form an impression in the minds of others that we do in fact practice what we preach. Our students are always watching us, and it is perhaps what we do in the hallways, in the cafeteria, and on the tennis courts that counts more than what we do from behind our desk or podium.

Prudent with Speech

Third, Gregory challenges us to *be prudent with our speech*. Seeking to find a balance between the active and contemplative, Gregory acknowledges that there is a time to keep silent and a time to speak boldly. "For just as reckless speaking leads someone into error," Gregory writes, "so indiscreet silence leaves in error those who might have been instructed" (*PR*, 2.4). On the one hand, many of us teachers seem to love hearing the sounds of our own voices, and the constant flow of speech flowing forth from our lips, if unguarded, can lead us to make statements that we regret. On the other hand, we can fail to speak up and insert our voices when they are most needed. Not only that, but we must be willing to have the courage to speak up when we hear (or, more likely, overhear) our students making comments that are demeaning or tearing others down rather than building others up. Some of my greatest teaching regrets, for instance, have come from not swiftly addressing head-on racist or sexist comments made by my students; as I have learned the hard way, to the extent that we fail to directly address such issues in our classroom, our moral authority suffers. We may hope to let students "work things out themselves" or want to avoid being that teacher who is the "morality police" interfering in our students' peer relationships. Ultimately, though, if we believe that taming the tongue is in fact a foundational element of Christian discipleship, we have no choice but to find "teachable moments" whenever and wherever we are able. Perhaps, if we are honest, we are more concerned with avoiding conflict or getting through the day's lesson plan than fulfilling the vocation given to us by God, who has entrusted us with the work of forming students' souls. Is it any wonder, then, that James's admonition to teachers (Jas 3:1) is immediately followed by his exhortation to tame the tongue (Jas 3:2–12)?

Healthy Boundaries

Fourth, we are to *set boundaries to our compassion*. Gregory's concern for balance here manifests as the need for spiritual leaders to be both filled with genuine, deep compassion for others and able not to get so caught up in the needs of others that they lose sight of their own relationship with God. "Otherwise," Gregory comments about such a person, "in pursuing high things he will despise the infirmities of his neighbors, or by adapting himself to the infirmities of his neighbors he will abandon the pursuit of high things" (*PR*, 2.5). The love of neighbor and the love of God, while always related, must nevertheless remain somewhat distinguished, lest an exclusive focus on one lead to the exclusion of the other. While it is unlikely that many teachers are so "heavenly minded" that they neglect the students in front of them, it may certainly be the case that there are some who have become so cynical or jaded towards their students, or so weighed down by tasks and responsibilities, that compassion and empathy are entirely lacking. Conversely, some teachers who exhibit an unhealthy, undifferentiated excess of concern for their students might in fact be engaging in efforts at spiritual activity apart from genuine spiritual rootedness in Christ. Like Christ removing himself from the crowds to go to the mountainside to pray, our concern for others and our ministry on their behalf must be nourished and sustained by those times of withdrawal and separation where we cultivate our inner lives with the Lord (Luke 6:12). Indeed, as Gregory goes on to elaborate, by nourishing our own souls, we are able to hear about and respond to the temptations and sins of others without ourselves falling into those traps. We can, therefore, establish healthy boundaries with our students such that we are truly invested in their lives, even as we find our sense of worth and source of empowerment for ministry in Christ alone.

Appropriate Discipline

Fifth, Gregory implores us to *exercise authority and discipline appropriately*. The spiritual leader, Gregory writes, must be appropriately humble on account of the fact that all humans are created equal by God. But on account of varying progress in virtue, God chose to ordain spiritual leaders for the good of others; these leaders, therefore, "should revel not in ruling over others but in helping them" (*PR*, 2.6). Gregory's main concern in this section is that spiritual authority may lead to pride, and therefore it is incumbent upon those in such positions of authority "to be careful that when they attack sin through due discipline, they should still acknowledge themselves, as an exercise of humility, to be the equals of those they correct" (*PR*, 2.6). This has interesting ramifications for conversations about student discipline. There are, of course, some teachers who avoid exercising their authority to discipline students out of a misguided desire to be "friends" with their students. Gregory, though, takes it as a given that being in a position of spiritual leadership will entail discipline, as even those who are not afraid of God or eternal damnation may turn from sin out of fear of human authority and earthly consequences. He is, therefore, more concerned with the spirit that lies behind the work of discipline, something that we can apply to both explicit moral correction and enforcement of school rules. Indeed, while it is imperative that we reproach and correct students when they miss the mark, we must always do so from a humble posture, recognizing that, like us, our students are created in the image of God; just as "the Lord disciplines the one he loves" (Heb 12:6), our motivation and our method of discipline must be grounded in humility and love.[22] The best defense against

---

22. As Gregory puts it later in this section (*PR*, 2.6), returning to his physician metaphor, "Indeed, it is necessary that whoever directs the healing of wounds must administer with wine the bite of pain and with oil the caress of kindness, so that what is rotten may be purged by the wine and what is curable may be soothed by the oil."

the insidious pride that threatens the exercise of godly discipline, Gregory insists, coming back to a theme that we are coming to recognize as central to his theology, is the difficult work of cultivating an internal life that overflows into an external life capable of being an attractive witness to those around us. As Gregory puts it, "any external show of authority must be balanced by an equal measure of internal subjugation" (*PR*, 2.6). Only then can we speak the truth in love (Eph 4:15), having the proper balance of being both gentle and firm in our discipline, a notion to which Gregory will return in his discussion on spiritual direction.

Active-Contemplative Balance

Sixth and finally, stating explicitly what has undergirded all that he has written so far, Gregory insists on *balancing the active and the contemplative*. A spiritual leader, he writes, "should not reduce his attention to the internal life because of external occupations, nor should he relinquish his care for external matters because of his anxiety for the internal life" (*PR*, 2.7). As discussed above, it is surely the case that as Christian educators in our time we need to heed the former advice much more often than the latter. Thus, we are like those of whom Gregory comments, "while they rejoice in being busied by worldly happenings, they remain ignorant of the internal life that they should have been teaching to others" (*PR*, 2.7). In our society, our frantic pace of life can serve as a status symbol by which our "complaints" about our busyness are really attempts to demonstrate to others—and perhaps to ourselves—our significance and worth.[23] But the cost of such a way of life, as Gregory is keen to remind us yet again, is to miss out on the work of self-examination and spiritual discipline needed to sustain and empower our Christian witness. As Eugene Peterson asks, "How can I lead people into the quiet place beside the still waters if I am in perpetual motion?"[24] We can deliver the most stimulating lectures, facilitate the most engaging discussions, and generate the most creative assessments, but if we have not a rich interior life that overflows with the love of God, we are, as Paul might say, noisy gongs and clanging cymbals (1 Cor 13:1). Gregory's contention is that only this active-contemplative balance, characterized especially by continual meditation on Scripture (*PR*, 2.11), will produce the kind of character that will allow the Christian leader to go about the work of spiritual direction (on which see the next section of this chapter). For only this kind

23. Purves rebukes those Christian leaders who are "compulsively and codependently driven to overwork" (Purves, *Pastoral Theology*, 71).

24. Peterson, *Contemplative Pastor*, 19; cf. Ps 23:2.

of person, Gregory insists, is capable of steering a course of moderation between laxity and severity (*PR*, 2.8), rightly discerning between virtue and vice (*PR*, 2.9) and meting out appropriate discipline (*PR*, 2.10).

As noted above, the first step towards integrating our inward motivations and our outward actions is to engage in the process of self-examination. Now that we have worked through this list of qualities that demonstrate such integration, we can begin considering how, practically speaking, we can apply these insights to our work as teachers. Specifically, I want to suggest that engaging with the Examen, meditation, and "soul friends" can bring alignment between our internal life and our external witness.

Examen

First, the prayer of Examen can be an effective tool for beginning or deepening our capacity for reflective self-examination. Though the specific form of this exercise is attributed to Ignatius of Loyola (1491–1556), its spirituality is essentially Gregorian. Simply put, the Examen is a way of prayerfully reflecting on the day, looking for God's presence and direction as well as engaging with our feelings and emotions. To pray the Examen, find a quiet place where you can be still and comfortable, and proceed to pray through the following five steps:[25]

(1) Gratefulness	(2) Invitation	(3) Examination	(4) Contrition	(5) Resolution
Become aware of God's presence, thanking him for who he is and for all of his gifts to you today.	Invite God to give you insight and illumination as you prepare to examine your day.	Walk through your day, considering both ways you moved towards God and ways you moved away from him.	Ask God for forgiveness, repenting of your sins and experiencing his grace and love.	Ask God for the strength to amend your ways and for his help in the day to come.

All of this usually takes no more than ten or fifteen minutes, but it does require a commitment to what Peterson calls "a deliberate withdrawal from the noise of the day, a disciplined detachment from the insatiable self."[26] While I heartily commend the Examen as a general spiritual discipline, as teachers we might find that this could be a particularly helpful tool for reflecting on our day in the classroom. What if, at the end of each school

---

25. This overview of the steps of the Examen is adapted from Warner, *Journey with Jesus*, 30. For a simplified version to use with children, see Paris, *Teach from the Heart*, 10–11.

26. Peterson, *Contemplative Pastor*, 20.

day, before rushing out of the building with papers to be graded in hand, we reserved a few minutes for praying the Examen over our time at work? How might this process of Spirit-directed reflection, over time, gradually bring integration to our inner lives and our external witness? The easiest objection, of course, is that there is simply not time for this. Peterson suggests simply scheduling time for such reflection on our calendars just as we would any other meeting or event; we will still have to accomplish the evening's grading, but perhaps we could be enlivened to go about it without becoming "harassed and anxious, a whining, compulsive Martha instead of a contemplative Mary."[27] Perhaps this would help us be a better spouse, parent, or caretaker when we return home from work. And, perhaps, we could go about our work the following day with a renewed sense of clarity, purpose, and integrity.

Meditation

Second, Gregory's insistence that spiritual leaders be "ever meditating in their hearts on the sacred Scriptures" (*PR*, 2.11) challenges us to make time amidst our busy schedules for not just prayerful self-examination but also soaking in the word of God. While most Christian educators are undoubtedly familiar with the notion of a morning "quiet time," I would like to suggest that more frequent rhythms of spiritual practices may be uniquely suited to aiding the teacher's spiritual life. Ultimately what we need is not a few minutes compartmentalized away at the start of the day but rather what Peterson describes as "a contemplative life adequate to our vocation," lest "the very work we do and our very best intentions, insidiously pride-fueled as they inevitably become, destroy us and all with whom and for whom we work."[28] As Peter Scazzero explains of his own life, "Within a couple of hours after being with God in the morning, I easily forgot God was active in my everyday affairs. By lunch I was grumpy and short with people. By late afternoon God's presence had disappeared from my consciousness."[29] How many class periods does it take until you lose sight of God's presence with you in your classroom? Perhaps it doesn't even survive that first frustrating faculty meeting before the start of school!

What might be more "adequate" for the demands of our work as Christian teachers, I propose, is a more regular pattern of setting aside time throughout the day to reset or refocus on the Lord, choosing to take time

27. Peterson, *Contemplative Pastor*, 23; cf. Luke 10:38–42.

28. Peterson, *Under the Unpredictable Plant*, 114.

29. Scazzero, *Emotionally Healthy Spirituality*, 141.

to meditate on him and his word even amidst all of our busyness. While the monastic pattern of stopping work for times of reading Scripture and prayer a full seven or eight times in a twenty-four-hour period may be beyond our present capacities, even finding a second or third time to stop, center ourselves, keep silence, and pray Scripture could pay dividends for our spiritual lives.[30] If we are to keep sight of our true purpose as Christian educators, amidst the daily demands, difficulties, and even dangers of our work, we have to press into Paul's charge to "pray without ceasing" (1 Thess 5:17), or what Peterson calls "recollected prayer."[31] How, though, can we practically do this? The possibilities to incorporate spiritual practices throughout our day are truly limitless.

One simple but powerful idea would be to pray through the midday office from the *Book of Common Prayer* during lunch.[32] Another would be to slowly and prayerfully meditate on a passage of Scripture using the ancient practice of *lectio divina*. In this form of spiritual reading of the Bible, we aim not just to understand words on a page but to have our lives permeated and transformed by the word of God. Traditionally, *lectio divina* consists of prayerfully engaging a short passage of Scripture through the following four steps:[33]

(1) Lectio	(2) Meditatio	(3) Oratio	(4) Contemplatio
Read and reread the text, slowly and carefully, paying attention to a word or phrase that stands out.	Repeat and reflect on that word or phrase, engaging your imagination, senses, and emotions.	Respond to the text with prayer, pouring your heart out in conversation with God.	Rest completely in God's presence, thanking him for meeting you in this time.

Christ's exhortation to "ask, and it will be given to you; seek, and you will find; knock, and it will be opened to you" (Matt 7:7) invites us to press into these practices, confident that the Lord will meet us as we seek his face. In so doing, we will increasingly become the kinds of people capable of being the spiritual leaders that our students so desperately need.

---

30. See Scazzero, *Emotionally Healthy Spirituality*, 139–63.

31. Peterson, *Under the Unpredictable Plant*, 106.

32. See Anglican Church, *Book of Common Prayer*, 33–39.

33. This overview of the steps of *lectio divina* is adapted from Warner, *Journey with Jesus*, 35. See further Peterson, *Eat This Book*, 81–117.

Soul Friends

Finally, if we are serious about growing in the qualities that will make us effective spiritual leaders in the classroom, we need to acknowledge our need for one another. The New Testament knows nothing of a "solo Christian"; rather, "in one Spirit we were all baptized into one body" (1 Cor 12:13). Our active participation in the worship of the local church is undoubtedly the primary place that we will realize our position in the body of Christ (Heb 10:19–25). While they cannot and must not replace the local church, our educational institutions can nevertheless be important sources of Christian community and encouragement for our specific task of walking out our calling of shepherding students' souls. To this end, we need what the Celtic Christians termed an *anam cara*, a "soul friend," with whom we can be in spiritually meaningful and vulnerable relationship.[34] Even a single spiritual friendship with a fellow teacher or staff member, characterized by a shared commitment to walking together intentionally on the paths of growth into Christ's likeness, can pay dividends for the soul. From breaking bread together to meeting before school for prayer and encouragement, opportunities to connect in meaningful and transformative ways, such that "iron sharpens iron" (Prov 27:17), not only boost our own spiritual growth but serve as powerful models for our students.

THE ART OF SPIRITUAL DIRECTION

Having examined the qualifications and qualities of a spiritual leader, we can now turn to Gregory's conception of the actual work of such a leader. Drawing again from the world of the monastery (not to mention the philosophical schools of antiquity, which emphasized how the purpose of rhetoric was the guidance of souls),[35] Gregory envisioned the Christian leader as a spiritual father who helped guide the spiritual growth of his subordinates or disciples—that is, what we might in the present day call the work of *spiritual direction*.[36] Just as Gregory's description of the art of spiritual direction helped priests and bishops of his day see themselves as more than just administrators or supervisors, it can likewise fire our imagination for a more transcendent understanding of our vocation as Christian educators.

The concept of spiritual direction, it is important to note, makes sense only in light of a proper understanding of the nature of the Christian life.

34. See O'Donohue, *Anam Cara*, xviii.

35. See Rylaarsdam, *John Chrysostom*, 19.

36. See Demacopoulos, *Gregory the Great*, 57–58.

For Gregory, and indeed early Christianity in general, the process of sanctification—of becoming more like Christ—is one that is long, arduous, and gradual; true disciples are generally moving forward on the path of progress in the spiritual life, and yet the reality of persistent sin and even spiritual regression is such that "the discerning eye of a spiritual mentor" is needed to keep the disciple on a trajectory of growth.[37] As teachers, we are in a unique position to provide such a discerning eye for at least some students; after all, it is entirely possible that we have more contact hours with them than they do with their parents, coaches, or pastors. Over the course of an academic year (or, sometimes, multiple academic years), we can observe so much about our students: the trivial things, of course, like their favorite snacks, fashion sensibilities, and romantic interests, but also the deeper things, such as their learning styles, insecurities, and heartbreaks. Moreover, as teachers we have frequent opportunities to share spiritual truth with our classes or even engage in significant conversations with our students that lend themselves to more intentional spiritual direction. Given, then, that we have the responsibility and the opportunity to help form our students' souls, Gregory's insights regarding spiritual direction prove surprisingly applicable, both at the general level of how we approach our classes and at the specific level of relationships with individual students.

We begin with a consideration of spiritual direction as applied to classes as a whole. At the outset of book 3 of his *Pastoral Rule*, Gregory summarizes his approach to spiritual direction with a compelling analogy (*PR*, 3.prol.):

> For example, what often helps some people will cause harm in others, just as herbs that are nutritious to some animals will kill others or the way that gentle hissing will calm a horse but excite a puppy. Likewise, the medicine that cures one disease will spur another, and the bread that fortifies a grown man can kill a young child. Therefore, the discourse of the teacher should be adapted to the character of his audience so that it can address the specific needs of each individual and yet never shrink from the art of communal edification. . . . And so every teacher, in order to edify all by the single virtue of charity, ought to touch the hearts of his audience with the same common doctrine but by distinct exhortations.[38]

37. Demacopoulos, *Gregory the Great*, 58; cf. *PR*, 2.8: "Of course, no one lives who does not sin occasionally." Though not the topic of this section, it is worth pointing out that this is the reason why we too need mentors or spiritual directors to guide us in our own lives.

38. Gregory's use of the physician metaphor hearkens directly back to his description

Just as the preacher Gregory describes in this passage has to consider how to teach a "common doctrine" with "distinct exhortations" in light of the mixed audience before him, our job as Christian teachers is to reach all of our students with "communal edification" and yet to do so in a way that recognizes the real differences among our students. To appropriate the jargon of the education world, we need to rightly *differentiate* our spiritual leadership in the classroom in light of the diverse body of learners under our care.

This starts, at the most basic level, with learning to truly *see* the students God has entrusted to us. We need to become, in other words, students of our students, at least at a general level—their hopes and dreams, their fears and anxieties, their virtues and vices. We can safely assume that our students are all on unique spiritual journeys, having been shaped by different familial, cultural, socioeconomic, racial, and religious contexts, and indeed having been further formed by distinct life experiences, giftings, traumas, and relationships. How, though, can we teach in such a way that edifies all of our students, in light of such diversity? Without knowing the intimate details of every student's life, how can we be sure that we are reaching all of the learners in our room?

Part of Gregory's genius was his articulation of thirty-six pairs of qualities that spiritual leaders should be sure to differentiate between. These include such obvious pairings as men and women, young and old, and poor and rich (*PR*, 3.2), as well as more nuanced, sophisticated opposites such as "those who bewail their sins but do not cease in committing them, and those who cease but do not bewail past sins" (*PR*, 3.30) or "those who do not begin good works, and those who begin but complete few of them" (*PR*, 3.34). What is particularly helpful about the list of binaries that Gregory provides, even if they can feel reductive at times, is that it suggests some broad categories of differences in people that can inform our understanding of our students even without knowing the specific circumstances of every student seated in our classroom. Males and females, auditory and visual learners, extroverts and introverts—our students are a diverse bunch. Even siblings can be very different from one another. Recognizing the many levels of differences among our students will help us keep this insight in mind if we are to design the kinds of spiritually formative learning experiences described later in this book.

To give just one example of how awareness of these categories might impact instructional design, in my context, in the American South, perhaps the most significant binary for my classroom is the presence of both white

---

of pastors as "physicians of the heart" in *PR*, 1.1. There are many instances of such metaphors being applied to philosophical rhetoric as far back as Plato and Aristotle; see Rylaarsdam, *John Chrysostom*, 19.

and black students. While we of course want to see each student uniquely apart from race, Gregory's approach helps us realize, for instance, that we should give careful consideration to the fact that our students of color may likely have very different opportunities, life experiences, and "social imaginaries" than our white students.[39] In working with my black students, then, I need to be careful not to assume certain experiences, viewpoints, and concerns that I find "normal" as a white person. For instance, asking my students to complete a family genealogy assignment for an American history class might be received differently by my African-American students who, because of the history of slavery in this country, might not be able to trace their lineage more than a few generations back. By carefully considering how my instruction or assignments will land differently with different groups of students, I can work towards making my teaching equally accessible to all my students and avoiding things that might put up needless barriers between my students and the spiritually formative goals that I have for them.

Diagnosis

While differentiation helps us to consider how to engage large groups of people as a spiritual leader, the heart of spiritual direction has always been in one-on-one relationships between the director and their disciple. Thankfully, as teachers we are not called to be spiritual directors to all of our students; after all, even Jesus focused on only twelve disciples (and within that group gave additional attention to only three).[40] But while we have the opportunity to reach all of our students with the kinds of spiritually formative teaching that will be unpacked later in this book, it is nevertheless the case that we will very likely be called to engage more intentionally with at least a few students each year. Whether a student shares a struggle or family concern with us during office hours or a student is brought before us regarding a discipline issue, opportunities for spiritual direction are inevitably there for the taking. How, though, can we best utilize these opportunities to point our students to Christ and his kingdom?

39. On Taylor's notion of the "social imaginary," see further J. Smith, *Desiring the Kingdom*, 65–71. As Smith defines it, "A social imaginary is not how we *think* about the world, but how we *imagine* the world before we ever think about it; hence the social imaginary is made up of the stuff that funds the imagination—stories, myths, pictures, narratives" (*Desiring the Kingdom*, 66; italics in original).

40. One advantage of working in a Christian institution or at least alongside other Christian colleagues is that different teachers following this same approach will inevitably reach different students, simply on account of their different ages, genders, personalities, denominational backgrounds, etc.

Gregory sets forth two major movements in the work of spiritual direction. The first step is to *diagnose* what is happening in a person's spiritual life. To do so effectively requires discernment.[41] This central element of Gregory's pastoral thought, George Demacopoulos explains, "is both the spiritual mechanism by which the master understands the needs of his disciples and the map onto which he charts the course for spiritual progress."[42] Beginning with the first of these elements, discernment is necessary if we are to look past outward appearances to the interior reality of others' spiritual conditions. Gregory contends, for example, that certain vices "lie hidden and require keen investigation so that their symptoms may be brought to light. The spiritual director must know these great vices by their small signs, and he must investigate the hidden thoughts of his subordinates and then intervene with the proper rebuke before it is too late" (*PR*, 2.10). The necessity of careful discernment is further underscored by the fact that many vices may appear as virtues (*PR*, 2.9), potentially threatening to upend our initial impressions of some of our students. That student we describe with glowing adjectives like "driven" and "self-motivated" might, if we look more closely, be better described as a "workaholic" or "perfectionist." The student who refuses to participate in the riotous behavior of his peers might in fact be motivated by pride and self-righteousness rather than the pursuit of virtue. In sum, if we are to be true physicians of the soul, we must be able to correctly diagnose what is going on in the souls of our students. But how do we go about this?

Like the work of self-examination, discernment is not easy. While we may simply pray that God gives us this gift, in the context of the broader *Pastoral Rule* it seems clear that the path to developing this gift requires our engagement with the spirituality of active contemplation that Gregory has returned to time and again in this work.[43] Moreover, simple practice can deepen our capacity for discernment. While Gregory certainly believed that discernment was a gift from God,[44] the physician metaphor helps us see that cultivating knowledge (such as the kinds of illnesses and remedies that exist) and virtue (such as the courage to perform a risky operation), as well as gaining expertise through repeated practice (which presumably includes both successes and failures), can contribute to the growth of one's capacity for discernment. Besides this, however, it also requires knowing our

41. On the roots of this understanding of discernment (*discretio*) in the thought of Benedict of Nursia and other monastic leaders, see Raab, "Gregory, Marmion," 32–33.

42. Demacopoulos, *Gregory the Great*, 72.

43. Raab, "Gregory, Marmion," 34: "*Discretio* does not stand alone, however. Its application requires the development of other related capacities." For example, "If compassion is needed, directors must also have cultivated their own wells of empathy."

44. See Demacopoulos, *Gregory the Great*, 72.

students at the heart level. Again, this may feel overwhelming, and the best place to start simply might be to focus on forging strong relationships with a few students each year. By showing up at their sporting events and dance recitals, joining them for trivia night at the local pizzeria, or inviting them to special worship services at our churches, we will be creating opportunities where real conversations will take place organically and appropriately.[45]

When these conversations arise, as they inevitably will, we may be relieved to find that it is not so much our theological acumen as our active listening skills that will convey our care and help us find a path forward in the conversation. In these moments, it is imperative that we give our students the gift of our undivided attention (something we likely could all stand to give more of to those we love), being fully present and seeking to truly understand the other person.[46] As the conversation continues, in the power of the Holy Spirit we can gently probe to discern what is going on below the surface of the student's life and identify what spiritual maladies might be at work in the soul. Harold Senkbeil encourages us to explore four dimensions of the spiritual life, each of which we can subtly interrogate in order to "attentively discern not just the symptoms of spiritual distress, but their underlying causes."[47] To this end, some relevant questions we might want to explore may include the following:[48]

Faith	Providence	Holiness	Repentance
Do you believe on the name of the Lord Jesus for salvation?	Can your faith handle adversity and reversals?	Do you regard God as holy and have appropriate fear of him?	Do you regard yourself as a sinner who is accountable to God?
Have you been baptized?	Do you believe that all things work together for those who love God?	Are you aware of what God demands from his followers?	Are there particular sins that you need to confess to someone?
What idols in your life are competing with your worship of the true God?	Do you, deep down, really believe that God is good?	Do you believe that God's holiness is available to us by faith in Jesus?	Are you able to accept God's forgiveness for your sins?

45. We should not discount the many possibilities for discipleship to take place in such informal settings: "'Come and see' was the pedagogy of Jesus. The truest learning is incarnational; we learn the deepest lessons looking 'over the shoulder' and 'through the heart,' seeing that a worldview can become a way of life" (Garber, *Fabric of Faithfulness*, 19).

46. See Senkbeil, *Care of Souls*, 68–69.

47. Senkbeil, *Care of Souls*, 91.

48. Adapted from Senkbeil, *Care of Souls*, 80–91.

Yes, we may have missed the chance to grade a few more essays or tweak next period's activity, but we have laid the foundation, through our patient, active, and intentional listening, for the work of spiritual direction.[49]

Treatment

In this second step of the process of spiritual direction, discernment not only enables us to diagnose accurately what is truly going on in a student's life, but it also empowers us to provide an individualized *treatment* for spiritual growth. Thus Gregory envisions the spiritual director, having made his diagnosis as best he can, delivering the right message, at the right time, in the right way.[50] Returning to the physician metaphor, Gregory explains that some injuries "are made worse by untimely surgery, and if a medicine is not suited to a certain situation, it would not be profitable to use it" (*PR*, 2.10). To make matters more complicated, what might be encouraged in one student might need to be rebuked in another; what might need to be addressed with one student might need to be overlooked in another who has more pressing issues with which to deal.[51] Even if we have an accurate diagnosis, how can we provide an appropriate treatment?

Thankfully, we are not ultimately the ones treating a student's spiritual needs; it is God himself, of course, who is the source of all true comfort and healing.[52] Our greatest treatment plan will always be to connect our students with the triune God who alone can bind up their wounds and mend their brokenness. Thus, despite the great diversity of spiritual maladies present in our students' lives, we can rest assured that we will never fail as spiritual directors if we focus on "enabling the soul to hear the word it needs in the context of its distress."[53] Where further discernment comes in, then, is knowing which word from God to speak in light of the prior diagnosis, carefully taking into account the spiritual needs of the individual.[54] What if, then, we approached every student interaction with an attitude of prayerful intention (perhaps making a habit of saying a prayer leading into each such

49. On what has been called the "ministry of small talk," see further Peterson, *Contemplative Pastor*, 111–16.

50. Raab, "Gregory, Marmion," 34; cf. Senkbeil, *Care of Souls*, 67; Purves, *Pastoral Theology*, 73–74; Peterson, *Contemplative Pastor*, 121.

51. This aspect of Gregory's approach to spiritual formation that calls for flexibility in the mentor's response to various disciples is known as *condescensio*; see further Demacopoulos, *Gregory the Great*, 73–74.

52. See Senkbeil, *Care of Souls*, 92–93.

53. Senkbeil, *Care of Souls*, 97.

54. See Senkbeil, *Care of Souls*, 98–99.

conversation), seeking to discern by the power of the Holy Spirit what is really going on in the life of that student and what word from God we could speak to assist that student on their journey? What if we were willing to take some risks, put ourselves out there a bit, and see what doors God might open? True, our attempts to forge meaningful connections with our students might be rejected or misunderstood, but such things even happened to the Lord, who promised the same for his followers (John 15:20). And there certainly may be times when our students' needs will outstrip our own abilities and qualifications, and the best thing we can do is to make a referral to a professionally trained pastor, therapist, or counselor. But simply by asking these questions, we are well on our way to recovering a crucial aspect of our vocation as Christian teachers. As Christian teachers, we are to do all aspects of our work with professionalism, expertise, and integrity, but perhaps our most distinctively Christian opportunity is to make the most of the ordinary interactions of our school day as the means by which we shape our students into Christ's likeness.[55] As argued above, we cannot be content with student mastery of content standards and skills, nor even with transmitting an accurate understanding of theology or a Christian worldview; ultimately, we aim to invite our students into an understanding of the good life as centered on Christ and his kingdom, into "the unending warfare against sin and sorrow and the diligent cultivation of grace and faith."[56] The art of spiritual direction gives us, therefore, an expanded imagination for the kind of work that will suffice for such a significant task. We can go about this task with courage, knowing that God is already at work in the lives of our students; we are merely looking to "discern how we can get in on it at the right time, at the right way."[57] Indeed, as Peterson helps us to see, "We have, of course, much to teach and much to get done, but our primary task is to be."[58] How many minutes of our work days, if we are honest with ourselves, are devoted to simply "being with" our students, to engaging them in conversation and prayer? What if we measured the quality of our days not by how much we "got done," but rather by the amount of unhurried, prayerful interactions we had with students who may not otherwise have any such adult interactions

55. The use of everyday moments as opportunities for discipleship is at the heart of Peterson's understanding of spiritual direction: "a way of life that uses weekday tasks, encounters, and situations as the raw material for teaching prayer, developing faith, and preparing for a good death" (*Contemplative Pastor*, 59).

56. Peterson, *Contemplative Pastor*, 56.

57. Peterson, *Contemplative Pastor*, 61. The language of discernment with respect to the appropriate time and way to go about the cure of souls is a clear echo of Gregory's *discretio*.

58. Peterson, *Contemplative Pastor*, 63.

in their lives? To the extent that we may not be satisfied with our present answers to these questions, we at least have a starting point from which we can consider how we might make room for these kinds of interactions going forward.

THE TEACHER, REIMAGINED

In this chapter, with the help of Gregory the Great and some present-day heirs of his approach to pastoral work and spiritual formation, we have reimagined what it means to be a teacher through the lens of spiritual direction. As Gregory's intense set of qualifications and characteristic qualities of such a person indicate, the work of spiritual direction can flow only out of a life soaked in an awareness of God's presence and steeped in the practices of self-examination, prayer, and Scripture reading. As we become people who are ourselves increasingly operating in the power and the confidence of the Holy Spirit, we can approach our students with a posture of greater discernment, humbly seeking to understand each student's unique background, needs, and spiritual journey, as well as to provide some counsel for how he or she might grow as a person of faith and virtue. This is not, of course, to say that only the holiest, most pious, or most charismatic among us have any hope of discipling students. Thankfully, we have the Lord's promise that "if you have faith like a grain of mustard seed, you will say to this mountain, 'Move from here to there,' and it will move, and nothing will be impossible for you" (Matt 17:20). Even when what we have to offer God seems like it will not be enough, God can take it and multiply it for his purposes (John 6:5–13). Thus, we can take comfort in the knowledge that "the Spirit helps us in our weakness" (Rom 8:26).

As we have considered the work of spiritual direction, the student part of the teacher-student relationship has come increasingly into view. Given the challenge and significance of the task at hand, we will also need to reimagine the nature of our students just as we have reconsidered our own identity as teachers. It is to a deeper, more richly theological understanding of the nature of our students, then, that we turn in the next chapter.

Basically the teacher should be a genuine believer + an example of that to their students.

3

Who Are Our Students?

John Chrysostom and Embodied Learning

The assumptions we make about human nature have dramatic impacts on how we conceive of the educational process. The teacher who sees her students as Lockean blank slates will undoubtedly have a different set of goals, pedagogical practices, and classroom management policies than the teacher who sees his students more along the lines of Hobbesian savages. From a Christian perspective, we come into the classroom with the assumption that our students are created in the image of God (Gen 1:26–27), but beyond this simple fact it is often easier to take our cues on the nature of our learners from secular social science than to really wrestle with some of the more uncomfortable implications of biblical anthropology.[1] We need guides, therefore, to help revitalize our imagination for what presuppositions we should hold concerning our students. Having reconceived of the identity and work of the teacher through the lens of Gregory the Great's insights on contemplative practices and spiritual direction, we now turn to the other half of the teacher-student relationship to consider how the insights of the early church fathers might help us to reimagine the nature of our

1. This is not to say that all social science research on education is wrong; in fact, in light of Christian belief in common grace, we should indeed expect to find some elements of convergence between Christian principles and those derived from secular research. For an excellent proposal for how to engage with social scientific literature from a Christian perspective, see Trentham, "Reading the Social Sciences Theologically."

learners. While the Christian tradition offers no shortage of vantage points for helping us better understand our students, we will again focus on just one that has not received sufficient grounding in contemporary literature on Christian education: the student as a fully embodied learner whose spiritual formation (or mis-formation) is largely driven by various sensory inputs. To assist us in unpacking this distinctive approach to educational philosophy, and to clarify how it furthers our conception of the teacher as a spiritual director seeking to form disciples of Christ, we will take up one of the most intriguing early Christian texts on pedagogy, John Chrysostom's homily "On Vainglory and the Right Way for Parents to Bring Up Their Children."

John Chrysostom (ca. 349–407) lived, like Gregory the Great two centuries later, in a turbulent time. Despite Christianity's ascendancy across the Roman world, the Greek-speaking East into which Chrysostom was born remained thoroughly saturated in Hellenistic (Greek) culture.[2] As noted in the previous chapter of this book, Christianity's dramatic change of status in the empire following the conversion of Constantine accelerated the growth of monastic movements wherein Christians could pursue lives of self-denial, celibacy, and prayer. To this end, after completing his traditional, classical education, the young Chrysostom gave up his secular pursuits and spent six years in the mountains, where his increasingly rigorous devotion to asceticism led to long-term health issues.[3] Still, when Chrysostom returned to Antioch and to ministry within the church there, his preaching would draw upon not only the rhetorical training of his youth but also his continued convictions regarding asceticism; in fact, Chrysostom himself would continue to hold himself to the standards of a monk.[4] Intriguingly, this implied that the monastic ideal was therefore just as accessible to a married lay person as it was to a monk (at least in theory; one wonders how having young children, for instance, squares with a quiet life of prayer and contemplation!). In his own life, therefore, Chrysostom engaged in active ministry in the world while he "remained a monk in his heart," such that he continued to engage in ascetical practices to the greatest extent possible in his various ministry settings.[5] It is not difficult, then, to see the trajectory from Chrysostom in the late fourth century to Gregory and his ideal of the "active contemplative life" in the late sixth century.

---

2. See Mayer and Allen, *John Chrysostom*, 3–4; Laistner, *Christianity and Pagan Culture*, 5–8.

3. On Chrysostom's experience as a young ascetic, see further Kelly, *Golden Mouth*, 14–35.

4. See Kelly, *Golden Mouth*, 35.

5. Kelly, *Golden Mouth*, 35.

Indeed, like Gregory, Chrysostom found himself attempting through his ministry and his writings to bridge the monastic and secular worlds. In 398, Chrysostom was consecrated bishop of Constantinople, which had in 330 become the new imperial capital. In this seat of the empire's power, Chrysostom was plunged into a sea of political and ecclesiastical intrigue that would result in his being exiled twice, the second of which ended with his untimely death in 407.[6] His legacy, though, was guaranteed through the quality of his preaching, by which he earned the epithet "Chrysostom" (meaning "golden-tongued"); we now have written records of nearly one thousand of his sermons spanning his years in both Antioch and Constantinople.[7] For our purposes, we will focus on just one of these homilies, the aforementioned "On Vainglory."

Though we do not know the exact date of this sermon or where it was preached, these issues do not affect our interpretation in any substantial way.[8] In this lengthy homily, which originally may have been read to parents, among other parishioners, we find one of Chrysostom's most detailed discussions of his educational philosophy.[9] Given its subject matter and its very specific and practical applications, this homily stands as one of the most important—and yet often overlooked, given its Byzantine and not Western provenance—patristic contributions to the early development of Christian pedagogical theory.[10] In this chapter, we will first consider some of Chrysostom's foundational assumptions about the nature of students insofar as they impact the need for and purpose of education, and then in light of these assumptions examine the pedagogical ramifications of students' embodied natures, concluding finally with a consideration of the ultimate end to which students' learning points. Through Chrysostom's imaginative metaphors and practical applications for the work of teaching and learning, we will be inspired to see how reenvisioning our learners along these lines coheres with our new understanding of the teacher as a spiritual director seeking to form disciples of Christ.

6. On Chrysostom's later life, see further Mayer and Allen, *John Chrysostom*, 8–11; Kelly, *Golden Mouth*, 104–285.

7. See Mayer and Allen, *John Chrysostom*, 7.

8. For full discussion of these issues, see Laistner, *Christianity and Pagan Culture*, 75–84.

9. See Christou, "Raising an Athlete for Christ," 105–8.

10. See Christou, "Raising an Athlete for Christ," 106.

FOUNDATIONAL ASSUMPTIONS ABOUT STUDENTS

In the early part of his homily "On Vainglory," Chrysostom sets out some foundational assumptions about the nature of human beings that form the essential background for understanding his educational philosophy. By articulating his understanding of the fundamental problem of the human condition, the formative power of education, and the essentially embodied nature of learners, Chrysostom lays the groundwork for the metaphor that he will develop at length in the central portion of this homily and challenges us to think differently about our students.

The Problem of Weakness

At the very outset of the homily, Chrysostom introduces a first foundational theological insight about the nature of all human beings: our natural inclination towards "vainglory," which refers to what we might today call empty pride, narcissism, or conceit.[11] Vainglory, Chrysostom writes, is "like a wild beast," responsible for "bringing ruin on the entire body of the Church," for it "is tearing the single body asunder into many separate limbs and is disrupting love" ("Vain.," §1).[12] More provocatively, it is like "a spirit with a lovely face," a harlot dressed in the finest fashions who easily seduces a young man into her room where she "would confound the wretched intruder and, leaping upon him and gaining possession of his soul, would drive his mind to frenzy" (Vain.," §2). Simply put, Chrysostom sees vainglory as having fundamentally corrupted not just individuals but also the surrounding culture more generally. As he develops his argument, Chrysostom identifies the lust for a high social status, along with the resulting praise from others, as the ultimate basis for the pursuit of wealth and extravagance that corrupts society as a whole. This, then, is the true nature of vainglorious human beings: we are driven by materialism, conspicuous consumption, and concern with prestige and the opinions of others. The story of the human race is one full of those who were, like *The Great Gatsby's* Tom and Daisy, "careless people," who "smashed up things and creatures and then retreated back into their money or their vast carelessness, or whatever is was that kept them together, and let other people clean up the mess they had made."[13] To put it

---

11. On the theme of vainglory across all of Chrysostom's writings, see Laistner, *Christianity and Pagan Culture*, 134n1.

12. All quotations from "On Vainglory" are taken from the translation of Laistner.

13. Fitzgerald, *Great Gatsby*, 179.

bluntly: our students are sinners, and apart from Christ there is something "awry" between them and God.[14]

Indeed, as Chrysostom elaborates elsewhere, human nature is characterized by an essential "weakness" common to all human beings on account of sin and its consequences.[15] This is nothing less than his take on the foundational Christian doctrine of original sin. As traditionally formulated, writes theologian Dennis Okholm, the doctrine of original sin posits that "like a compass needle that always points north, our lives are inclined toward sin from the very beginning."[16] Despite the fact that orthodox Christian educators will almost all likely intellectually assent to this doctrine, in practice even "Christian" approaches to teaching and learning, especially those that uncritically adopt "student-centered" language that elevates students' autonomy and abilities with respect to their learning and capabilities, tend to work from a Pelagian framework that understands students as being able to choose the good freely apart from God's grace.[17] After all, as the Reformed tradition has helpfully articulated, the effects of the fall extend even to our cognitive abilities.[18] What is needed, then, is an approach to education that is neither "student-centered" nor "teacher-centered" but in fact truly "Christ-centered."

As Chrysostom helps us to see, our students today are likewise infected with the same virus of narcissism, fundamentally oriented from birth to desire and pursue status, wealth, and material luxuries. To compound matters, our consumer-driven capitalist economy is oriented around feeding and exploiting this very truth.[19] Even apart from those churches that teach an explicit prosperity gospel, so much of American Christianity has relegated Jesus to being an accomplice to the American dream or an avatar for Christian nationalism rather than the one who asks us, "For what does it profit a man to gain the whole world and forfeit his soul?" (Mark 8:36). The obvious implication, then, is that left unchecked, children will take on the

14. Peterson, *Contemplative Pastor*, 118.

15. This concept is developed by Chrysostom at, e.g., *On the Incomprehensible Nature*, 3.18; cf. Rylaarsdam, *John Chrysostom*, 16–17.

16. Okholm, *Learning Theology*, 144. While Chrysostom portrays the human will as weakened as if by sickness, the Western tradition tends to portray the will to do what is good as effectively dead; these differences are immaterial for the argument of this chapter, but for more detail see Okholm, *Learning Theology*, 150–51.

17. On Pelagianism, see Okholm, *Learning Theology*, 145–49.

18. On the noetic effects of original sin, see, e.g., Azadegan, "Divine Hiddenness and Human Sin"; Vandici, "Reading Rules of Knowledge."

19. The formative power of our cultural practices in this regard is perhaps best illustrated by James K. A. Smith's "liturgies of consumerism"; see J. Smith, *Desiring the Kingdom*, 93–103.

materialist values, consumerist habits, and political ideologies of their parents or the surrounding culture, especially if moral or spiritual formation is not considered a necessary part of a child's education. Thus, as Chrysostom reasons, "What will become of boys[20] when from earliest youth they are without teachers? If grown men, after being nurtured from the womb and continuing their education to old age, still do not live righteously, what wrong will not children, accustomed from the threshold of life to empty words, commit? In our own day every man takes the greatest pains to train his boy in the arts and in literature and speech. But to exercise this child's soul in virtue, to that no man any longer pays heed" ("Vain.," §18).

An education, Chrysostom here argues, is not just about the transmission of knowledge or the acquisition of skills; it is, in fact, also (and perhaps ultimately) about the formation of the soul.[21] This was, of course, a foundational principle of pagan education as well; across antiquity, we find that the greatest pagan teachers all argued that the central function of education was to provide moral training.[22] For Chrysostom, though, this cuts to the heart of what it means for parents to fulfill Paul's admonition to bring up children "in the discipline and instruction of the Lord" (Eph 6:4).[23] By adopting such an approach to education we will likely find ourselves at cross-purposes with many of our students and their families, many of whom may be more concerned with the future judgment of an admissions officer or employer rather than with Christ's. But if we are to be true to our vocation as Christian educators, we have no option but to keep our focus resolutely on the central task of forming students' souls despite our awareness of the overwhelming counter-formational pressures that students encounter simply by being a part of modern society.[24]

---

20. In Chrysostom's time, education was primarily the domain of young men from wealthy families, hence his reference to "boys" only. The fact that modern education is inclusive of both men and women does not, however, diminish the application of Chrysostom's ideas here.

21. See Christou, "Raising an Athlete for Christ," 111–12.

22. See Laistner, *Christianity and Pagan Culture*, 15. As succinctly put by Rylaarsdam (*John Chrysostom*, 13): "Classical *paideia* was the process of educating humans into their true form, their ideal human nature." On the failures of the modern educational system in this regard, see Palmer, *To Know as We Are Known*, 33–40.

23. As Chrysostom puts it in another homily: "This, then, is our task: to educate both ourselves and our children in godliness; otherwise what answer will we have before Christ's judgement-seat?" ("Homily Twenty-One," 71).

24. See, e.g., J. Smith, *Desiring the Kingdom*, 89–129.

Education as Formation

Thus far, Chrysostom has painted a rather bleak picture of human nature and its implications for our students. Thankfully, Chrysostom's next key presupposition points us to the fact that students' predispositions need not define their destiny. Rather, students are able to be shaped or molded by their education, trained to become people whose ways of thinking and living ultimately produce virtue.[25] This language of training comes through most clearly with Chrysostom's charge to parents and teachers to "raise up an athlete for Christ" ("Vain.," §19), suggesting that Chrysostom sees education as requiring consistent (and even painful at times!) exercise to condition the student to a life of disciplined virtue.[26] Chrysostom then develops the formational possibilities of education in a series of further metaphors. Thus, students' souls are akin to wax seals: "If good precepts are impressed on the soul while it is yet tender, no man will be able to destroy them when they have set firm, even as does a waxen seal" ("Vain.," §20).

Likewise, Chrysostom suggests later, students are like blocks of marble, being chiseled away by sculptors into wonderful works of art: "Sculptors, too, working in marble, proceed in a similar manner; they remove what is superfluous and add what is lacking. Even so must you proceed. Like the creators of statues do you give all your leisure to fashioning these wondrous statues for God. And, as you remove what is superfluous and add what is lacking, inspect them day by day, to see what good qualities nature has supplied so that you will increase them, and what faults so that you will eradicate them" ("Vain.," §22). While this metaphor seems to see students as only passive recipients of the work of spiritual formation, Chrysostom is nevertheless pointing out an important truth: that despite their weakness and proclivity for vainglory, young people are capable of being molded or formed in a different direction, into the image of Christ. Like Michelangelo, we can imagine ourselves as being called to the work of setting free the statue (that is, the student in all of her glory as Christ has created her to be) from the surrounding block of marble (that is, the sin that disfigures the *imago Dei* in her). This requires, though, an education that explicitly includes instruction in virtue and provides opportunities for students to exercise or train the "muscles" of their souls. It requires, in other words, a teacher who is committed to an understanding of the teaching vocation as explicitly *counter-formational* to the prevailing currents shaping students from both within and without. This is, I believe, what Paul was getting at

25. See Christou, "Raising an Athlete for Christ," 109–10.
26. See Christou, "Raising an Athlete for Christ," 109.

when he instructed the church at Rome, "Do not be conformed to this world, but be transformed by the renewal of your mind" (Rom 12:2). If our default is to conforming to the world's way of thinking and to pursuing our vocations as teachers from within the framework of anthropological presuppositions foreign and often contrary to Christian teaching, it will take nothing less than a renewed vision of the work of teaching and learning to see our students' transformation into Christ's likeness.

Embodied Learners

Finally, lest we imagine that his approach to education is concerned only with the immaterial nature of students' existence, Chrysostom makes a further crucial assumption about the nature of learners: they are fundamentally embodied beings. Following in the Platonic tradition, Chrysostom conceived of students, like all people, as having souls consisting of three parts: reason, spirit, and appetite ("Vain.," §65).[27] It is Chrysostom's development of the "appetitive" aspect of our students, which we will explore in more detail below in his metaphor of the student as a walled city, that is most relevant for this present study insofar as it helps us understand our students as having physical bodies by which they perceive the world.

This aspect of the ancient conception of human personhood has recently been popularized by James K. A. Smith. In his *Desiring the Kingdom*, Smith posits that "education is not something that traffics primarily in abstract, disembodied ideas; rather, education is a holistic endeavor that involves the whole person, including our bodies, in a process of formation that aims our desires, primes our imagination, and orients us to the world— all before we ever start *thinking* about it."[28] Echoing the Platonic tradition's insight that the appetitive aspect of human personhood is the seat of desire and the pursuit of pleasure, we are indeed what Smith calls "fundamentally desiring creatures."[29] Though Chrysostom may have used different terms and not made his point so explicitly, Smith's understanding of human

27. On this view's influence in early Christian theology, see Laistner, *Christianity and Pagan Culture*, 139n36. The great accomplishment of Chrysostom, according to Christou ("Raising an Athlete for Christ," 111), was that he "weaves together each of these aspects, seeking to articulate a holistic educational philosophy that addresses the human being as qualitatively diverse and complex." See further Plato, *Republic*, 4.439d–41a.

28. J. Smith, *Desiring the Kingdom*, 39–40 (italics in original).

29. J. Smith, *Desiring the Kingdom*, 40. While Smith primarily utilizes Augustine of Hippo to develop this point, Chrysostom would have been an equally illuminating point of entry for his discussion.

beings as "desiring animals" who "intend the world" through their "ultimate loves," powerfully shaped by their mundane habits and practices, seems to accurately summarize Chrysostom's own approach.[30]

With these basic assumptions about learners in place—their proclivity towards vainglory on account of human weakness, their potential for spiritual formation through education, and their essentially embodied existence—we can at last turn to one of Chrysostom's most powerful metaphors for education: the student's soul as a walled city, whose gates must be carefully monitored for the health of the city and whose citizenry must be governed through the careful writing and enforcement of laws. Walls, in Chrysostom's time, were the necessary defenses that secured the inhabitants of a city from the threats of the outside world; the gates of the walls, then, were the means by which outsiders came into the city and the inhabitants of the city exited into the outside world. The regulations specifying who could pass in and out of these gates would therefore be a central concern for any well-regulated city, and thus Chrysostom makes the need to carefully guard these gates the focus of this extended metaphor.

GUARDING THE GATES OF THE SOUL

In introducing the metaphor that will dominate the central portion of this homily, Chrysostom begins with the charge to the child's parent to "regard thyself as a king ruling over a city which is the soul of thy son; for the soul is in truth a city" ("Vain.," §23). An educated person at the time would hear in this statement a clear echo of Plato's *Republic*, which also utilized the metaphor of a city to develop Plato's understanding of the soul as having three parts.[31] While Chrysostom is clear that it is parents who are the ultimate authorities over their children, it is nevertheless the case that some aspect of this authority, in both Chrysostom's day and our own, is delegated to teachers who stand in for the parent in providing the child's education.[32] This takes some pressure off teachers insofar as the primary responsibility for a student's formation lies with his or her parents, and yet throughout the homily it is clear that Chrysostom sees the work of the teacher as possessing, by extension, this same authority. In light of his presuppositions concerning

30. For J. Smith's account of human personhood, see especially *Desiring the Kingdom*, 46–73.

31. See further Christou, "Raising an Athlete for Christ," 113; cf. Plato, *Republic*, 4.434d–36a.

32. The notion of *in loco parentis* continues to be an explicit hallmark of many covenantal Christian schools.

the essential weakness of human beings and the formative opportunities for teachers with respect to young people, it makes sense that Chrysostom would have a high and serious view of the work of a teacher. Though the previous chapter of this book emphasized the notion of the teacher as a spiritual director, Chrysostom's metaphor of the teacher as king over the city, we will come to discover, largely resonates with the approach outlined by Gregory the Great.

Within this city that is the child's soul, Chrysostom continues, there are a variety of citizens, corresponding to different thought processes, who in various ways can build up or undermine the general welfare of the city. As he explains, "even as in a city some are thieves and some are honest men, some work steadily and some transact their business fitfully, so it is with the thoughts and reasoning in the soul" ("Vain.," §23). This is where the teacher, as king over the city, finds his place; in this city of the child's soul, as in any other city, "we need laws to banish evildoers and admit the good and prevent the evildoers from rising up against the good" ("Vain.," §24). Just as a city without a strong ruler will devolve into anarchy and chaos, so the child's soul will succumb to her natural proclivity to vainglory without the presence of a caring but firm adult who can set appropriate limits and boundaries in her life.[33] Thankfully, as Chrysostom reminds us, recalling his assumption that students are able to be shaped or molded by their education, because the child's soul is like a city "but lately founded and built," it is "very easy to direct" ("Vain.," §25). Of course, as any teacher or parent knows, rules that are not enforced are not followed and end up undermining that adult's authority. As Chrysostom bluntly puts it, "it is useless to draw up laws, if their enforcement does not follow" ("Vain.," §26).[34]

What, though, are these laws with which the teacher should be concerned? Chrysostom devotes the bulk of the homily to emphasizing how the king of the city must regulate or control the flow of the citizens in and out of the city's outer walls, which Chrysostom identifies as the student's various senses. Chrysostom introduces this next portion of his metaphor with these words:

> Draw up laws, and do you pay close attention; for our legislation
> is for the world and today we are founding a city. Suppose that
> the outer walls and four gates, the senses, are built. The whole
> body shall be the wall, as it were, the gates are the eyes, the
> tongue, the hearing, the sense of smell, and, if you will, the sense

---

33. This is also a cornerstone of good parenting; cf. Mamalakis, *Parenting toward the Kingdom*, 150–95.

34. See further Mamalakis, *Parenting toward the Kingdom*, 196–249.

of touch. It is through these gates that the citizens of the city go
in and out; that is to say, it is through these gates that thoughts
are corrupted or rightly guided. ("Vain.," §27)

In pivoting to talk about the gates of the city, Chrysostom is suggesting that
each of a student's senses plays a distinct role in how he or she learns and
is formed into a particular kind of person.[35] As we will see, this requires us
to consider how we can provide a holistic education for the whole human
person, taking into account how each of the senses can be trained to pursue virtue.[36] Though some of the assumptions and practices of pedagogy in
Chrysostom's context may be quite foreign to those of our own day, giving
careful attention to the "gates" described in this homily helps us to consider
how our students' spiritual formation is impacted by their embodied nature. With this overview of the metaphor complete, we can now turn, with
Chrysostom, to consider the pedagogical significance of each of the gates,
or senses, in turn.

Speech

The first gate that Chrysostom discusses is the *gate of the tongue*. Chrysostom begins by noting that this gate is "the busiest of all," and is guarded with
doors and bolts fashioned of gold, which symbolize "the words of God" that
are to be on the lips of students at all times ("Vain.," §28). If the city (that
is, the child's soul) is in fact to be the dwelling place of the "King of the
universe," Chrysostom insists that we then consider what kind of citizens
should be transiting the city by this gate: "Of what character shall these citizens be? We must train the child to utter grave and reverent words. We must
drive many strangers away, so that no corrupt men may also find their way
in to mingle with these citizens. Words that are insolent and slanderous,
foolish, shameful, common, and worldly, we must expel. And no one save
only the King must pass through these gates" ("Vain.," §28).

The teacher, as the ruler of the city who is tasked with controlling its
population, therefore has a fundamental responsibility to disciple students
in line with Paul's injunction to "let no corrupting talk come out of your
mouths, but only such as is good for building up, as fits the occasion, that
it may give grace to those who hear" (Eph 4:29).[37] Chrysostom therefore

35. Chrysostom's connection between learning and the different senses anticipates
the modern notion of modalities of learning; cf. Littlejohn and Evans, *Wisdom and
Eloquence*, 169–71.

36. See Christou, "Raising an Athlete for Christ," 114.

37. Chrysostom himself cites a portion of this verse in "Vain.," §28.

returns to the image of the ruler's legislative powers, suggesting first of all a law that a student "speak ill of no man, that he swear not, that he be not contentious," using various forms of rewards and discipline to reinforce this outcome ("Vain.," §30).[38] This requires, Chrysostom suggests, the teacher to be vigilant in observing the student's speech towards others and to intervene to "stop his mouth from speaking evil" ("Vain.," §31). Recognizing the grand scope of this particular element of the child's formation, Chrysostom encourages the teacher to enlist other adults in the student's life to ensure that someone is always "on the watch" ("Vain.," §32). Before long, Chrysostom suggests, this habit of worthy speech will be "firmly established as his second nature" ("Vain.," §33) and "thus this gate will have been made worthy of the Lord" ("Vain.," §34), the city purged of its unworthy citizens ("Vain.," §35).

As we consider how we could apply this notion of guarding the gate of the tongue in the classroom, we may begin by reflecting on the enormous importance of the tongue for discipleship. As indicated throughout the Bible, but especially in the epistle of James, the tongue is powerful but very difficult to control; with it we both praise God and curse those made in God's image (Jas 3:3–12). As we discovered in the previous chapter from Gregory the Great, part of our own formation into Christ's likeness includes becoming prudent with our own speech. Beyond setting an example through our own habits of speech, we can follow Chrysostom in the recognition that instructing students in virtue will invariably involve training their speech. We can point our students to the wisdom found in the book of Proverbs, teaching them that "a gentle tongue is a tree of life, but perverseness in it breaks the spirit" (Prov 15:4) or that "a lying tongue hates its victims, and a flattering mouth works ruin" (Prov 26:28).[39] We can, moreover, set out clear expectations concerning speech in the classroom and utilize a variety of disciplinary strategies to motivate our students accordingly. Here it might be helpful to explicitly connect classroom expectations in this regard to the belief that each student is an image bearer; if we believe that our classroom is a community of image bearers collectively pursuing goodness, truth, and beauty, our commitments to how we talk to and about one another must reflect that reality. This extends especially to those conversations that touch on issues of politics or race that are causes for division and anger in our broader society. Perhaps inviting students to hold us accountable for

38. Perhaps surprisingly for his time, Chrysostom discourages corporal punishment as a means of discipline (though not the threat of it!) ("Vain.," §30).

39. I have found that Proverbs is particularly accessible for teenagers, with its very practical wisdom meeting students where they are at and setting up valuable contrasts with the "wisdom" of the world.

our own speech, as foreign as such an idea may have been in Chrysostom's context, might be part of building the kinds of relationships within which such spiritual transformation can take place. I actually foreground this in my syllabi distributed at the start of the year: after setting out the notion of our class as "a community of image bearers" and its implications, I state that "if you ever feel like there is something that I or another student is doing or saying that places a 'stumbling block' in your way, please let me know as soon as possible." Holding ourselves to the same standards as our students and opening ourselves to correction when necessary is, I believe, an important part of getting student buy-in on the expectations for classroom community.[40]

Beyond this, Chrysostom helps us to see that to truly accomplish this goal we have to be willing to admonish students regarding their interactions with one another as well as to include parents, coaches, and other influential adults in this broader project of training in virtuous speech. This seems to presuppose a certain level of engagement with our students such that we know them in the context of their peer and familial relationships. In other words, really training students in virtuous speech will involve relationships that transcend the four walls of the classroom, even if the classroom is the primary locus for this training.

Hearing

The second gate that Chrysostom analyzes is the *gate of the ear*, which he expounds upon at length. Comparatively, Chrysostom spends far more time on this gate than any of the other gates, reflecting its great significance for him. Whereas the gate of the tongue was one by which citizens could only exit, this gate is exclusively an entry point into the city; that is to say, here the focus is on the words that a student takes in rather than the words a student speaks. The two are, of course, related: "he that hears no base or wicked words does not utter base words either" ("Vain.," §36). Chrysostom is especially concerned with potentially unsuitable content that students could be exposed to in their lessons. Thus, students' educations should not include "frivolous and old wives' tales" ("Vain.," §38).[41] Rather, teachers should con-

---

40. Perhaps this classroom covenant needs to expand to include speech outside of the classroom itself; after all, so much of our students' impure speech is not spoken aloud in class but "spoken" via text or social media. This points to the need for thoughtful engagement with technology, which we will discuss as part of the gate of the eyes below.

41. Here Chrysostom alludes to the fact that the child's teacher is likely not his father but in fact a servant or a hired tutor, who is in either case a "virtuous man" ("Vain.," §38).

tinually seek to immerse their students in the stories of the Bible, such that the student's "soul is being formed thus by such tales" ("Vain.," §39).[42] The teacher, Chrysostom insists, should read these stories with full dramatic flair and with an eye to application for the development of virtue, coming back to them often so that they are "fixed in his memory" ("Vain.," §41).[43] The biblical stories taught to students should be age-appropriate, Chrysostom insists, saving more difficult or sobering texts for older children ("Vain.," §52). Thus, by keeping what is base away from students and instead focusing their attentions on the stories of Scripture, teachers will not only stop evil citizens from entering the city through the ear but also prevent the release of such citizens from the city through the tongue.

With his attention to the content of what students are learning, Chrysostom is encroaching on the subject of the next chapter of this book, and so we will leave a broader discussion of that subject until then. For now, though, we may note that while the emphasis on orality in passing along literature and tradition in the ancient world is different from today's focus on reading, we can still consider how the subject material to which we are exposing our students, as they "hear" it in their minds when reading, is essentially formative. Indeed, Chrysostom's first powerful insight here is that he correctly recognizes the formative nature of everything that students are hearing or reading. Teachers, who have an infinite amount of subject material to draw on, thus have the obligation to select texts and topics that are not "base" but can point students to lives of virtue and faith.

That our curriculum has the potential to either point toward what is good, beautiful, and true or point away from those things is perhaps best illustrated by considering the relationship between the gate of the ear and music. The ability of songs to "stick" in our heads is, of course, why it is so much easier to memorize words set to music than it is plain prose, a truth that is utilized by elementary school teachers and liturgical churches alike. Concerns about the possible negative effects of music extend at least as far back as Plato.[44] In our present day, we would be naïve to imagine that the music that students listen to, in their cars on the way to school,

---

42. Chrysostom highlights the stories of Cain and Abel (Gen 4:1–16; cf. "Vain.," §39–42) and Jacob and Esau (Gen 25:27; 27:1–38; cf. "Vain.," §43–44) as particularly helpful for teaching many important lessons. The same point is developed by Chrysostom in another of his homilies: "Let us give [children] a pattern to imitate; from their earliest years let us teach them to study the Bible" ("Homily Twenty-One," 67).

43. It is perhaps for the same reason that Chrysostom insists that parents name their children not after their forebears but rather after the saints of the church, thus by their names giving them "from the first an incentive to goodness" ("Vain.," §47).

44. See Plato, *Republic*, 4.424c.

as they do their homework, and as they walk the halls of campus (indeed, some students seem to pretty much *always* be listening to music), has no significant formative potential. So much of contemporary popular music, even apart from profanity and other forms of crudeness, explicitly articulates a worldview of self-gratification and self-centeredness. Perhaps helping our students cultivate an appetite for good and beautiful music (rather than pandering to their own likes in a misguided effort to be cool or relevant) is an underappreciated aspect of their spiritual formation. Rather than having students I am supervising in a study hall sit in silence, I often play music with a soothing, otherworldly feel—Gregorian chant, for instance. They may not like it, at least at this age, but widening their horizons by gradually exposing them to such things can expand their imagination for alternatives to the kinds of music that otherwise dominate their lives.

Beyond this, however, Chrysostom helps us to see the importance of stories in communicating truth about the Christian life, for stories have a way of planting seeds in our minds that "stick." As the philosopher Alasdair MacIntyre reminds us, "man is in his actions and practice, as well as in his fictions, essentially a story-telling animal."[45] There is a reason, of course, that Jesus himself taught in parables rather than in discourses on systematic theology. Therefore, Chrysostom's emphasis on teaching through stories, and helping our students find their place in God's broader story of creation, fall, redemption, and restoration, is very much an insight that we can draw on. Finally, Chrysostom's awareness of the need for differentiation and for selecting age-appropriate resources is a good reminder that the best application of his insights is always dependent on the particular group of students that we have in front of us. In sum, by attuning ourselves to our role as guardians of students' ears, we are challenged to give careful consideration to the material we are putting before our students. This is not to say, of course, that we should never select texts containing problematic content or issues, especially for older students, but even here there is a recognition that we must do so in a thoughtful way and with adequate support to help students process that content from a Christian perspective.[46]

Smell

The third gate that Chrysostom analyzes, albeit briefly, is the *gate of the nose*. While protecting our students from the literal smells they take in is almost certainly not an element of our current pedagogical concerns, Chrysostom insists

---

45. MacIntyre, *After Virtue*, 216.

46. See the following chapter of this book for an extended discussion of these issues.

that even this aspect of our students' embodied experience has ramifications for their formation in virtue and faith.[47] Here, Chrysostom is concerned with "perfume," for these sweet odors relax brain and body, and thereby "pleasures are fanned into flame and great schemes for their attainment" ("Vain.," §54). Thus, Chrysostom encourages teachers to help keep students from developing an attachment to the comforts and pleasures of this life. The influence of Chrysostom's ascetical theology on this point is clear: to combat students' innate orientation to desire wealth and material luxuries, only a rigorous plan of counter-formation (i.e., asceticism) can train the body, and indeed the soul, to desire the things of God above these things of the world.

Chrysostom's short reference to this gate is perhaps the most challenging for us as modern educators. Even if we admit that students are more than brains on a stick and fully affirm the importance of training students' tongues and guarding their ears, it is not easy to extend this line of thinking to the sense of smell. Saving a discussion of asceticism for our discussion of Chrysostom's fifth and final gate, we may therefore move to extend Chrysostom's point to encompass the metaphorical "scent" that each of us gives off or that permeates the classroom. After all, Paul reminds us that we are the "aroma of Christ" (2 Cor 2:15), using the metaphor of smell to illuminate how Christians are called to bring goodness and beauty into the world around them. Through this image, Paul is asking us to consider how, on the one hand, pleasant smells are life-giving, enticing, and draw people together, and how, on the other, unpleasant smells push people apart; Christians, then, are called to be the former and not the latter. We may, therefore, wish to help our students take stock of what "smell" they are giving off through their body language, attitude, and level of engagement, even as we can consider our own "scent" as it speaks to how students perceive our level of authenticity and approachability. Furthermore, in the Old Testament, smell was often associated with sacrifices and offerings, which had a pleasing aroma to the Lord.[48] Given, then, that in the new covenant we are to offer ourselves as living sacrifices (Rom 12:1), it is not a stretch to say that the work that we do in the classroom, students and teachers alike, has the potential to be a fragrant offering unto the Lord, especially as we use our gifts to build one another up in love (Phil 4:18). This points us to a broader discussion of classroom culture, which we will take up in more detail in chapter 5 of this book.

47. J. Smith (*Desiring the Kingdom*, 95n10) points out that "aroma marketing" is utilized by some stores to lure in shoppers and drive purchases, as scent is apparently closely linked with memory and therefore can be used to exploit feelings of nostalgia.

48. See, e.g., Gen 8:21; Exod 29:18; Lev 1:17.

Sight

The fourth gate Chrysostom presents is the *gate of the eyes*, which he de-scribes in some detail. Chrysostom concedes the eyes are particularly dif-ficult to guard, "since there burns a fire within and, so to speak, a natural corruption" ("Vain.," §60). Here he has in mind the particular problem of sexual immorality, and Chrysostom warns teachers against exposing their students to places like the theater ("Vain.," §56) or mixed-gender baths ("Vain.," §60) that could lead to arousal.[49] Rather, he insists, teachers should show students "the sky, the sun, the flowers of the earth, meadows, and fair books" as examples of pleasurable things for the eyes that are nevertheless "harmless" ("Vain.," §59). Like the patriarch Joseph, he argues, students should flee from sexual sin, and in so doing they will keep themselves pure for marriage ("Vain.," §61).[50] While this can for Chrysostom result in the rather extreme conclusion that the male student should "have no converse with any woman save only his mother" ("Vain.," §62), the notion of wanting to protect students from sexual temptation is of course readily applicable to our present day and age.

In our context, when we think of guarding students' eyes, especially in the context of protecting them from being exposed to sexual immorality, our thinking immediately goes to the issue of online pornography, and undoubt-edly rightly so. Indeed, as we continue to learn more about the pernicious effects of internet pornography or, more broadly, how technology addiction and social media are rewiring students' brains, Chrysostom's challenge to guard our students' eyes takes on more significance as we reflect on Christ's teaching that "the eye is the lamp of the body" (Matt 6:22). No technological device or tool is value-neutral; rather, all technology is formative insofar as it creates habits, promotes virtues (or vices), and inscribes certain views of the good life. That is to say, technology shapes not only the world but also the people in it, changing the ways that we think, relate, and act such that we are in danger of becoming less human.[51] Thus, while technology ideally shapes the world for redemptive purposes, if used uncritically or selfishly

49. While the mixed-gender baths likely need no explanation, the theater of late antiquity was a place of poor moral repute; Chrysostom alludes to "the sight of naked women uttering shameful words" as characterizing the theater of his day ("Vain.," §78).

50. Interestingly, Chrysostom seems to assume that the student will get married, hence the teacher's "promise" to guide him to a match with a "virtuous woman" ("Vain.," §61), rather than leaving the door open for a call to the monastic life and therefore celibacy. On the story of Joseph and Potiphar's wife, see Gen 39.

51. See further Postman, *Technopoly*; Crouch, *Tech-Wise Family*; Carr, *Shallows*; Dreher, *Benedict Option*, 218–36.

it can adversely impact our students' spiritual and intellectual formation. To this end, David Smith calls us to embrace "Christian discernment," asking educators to consider how the use of new digital technologies might affect students' relationships with God and with one another, as well as their impacts on students' moral and spiritual formation, among other things.[52] While responding to the challenge of modern digital technology far exceeds the scope of this book, it is clear that Christian educators seeking to guard their students' eyes must consider not just the *content* accessed by digital devices but also the *devices and programs themselves* that threaten to subvert our efforts at Christian formation.

As with the other gates Chrysostom has described thus far, this can best be accomplished through true partnership with students' families; keeping parents educated about the dangers of certain aspects of technology and the ways that they can partner with teachers to help guard their children's eyes is the only workable proposal for ensuring that the values and habits of the classroom are not subverted in the privacy of the student's home. Besides this, Chrysostom's positive injunction to direct students' eyes to what is beautiful and lovely can inspire our thinking about how to make our classrooms a "garden of delight" for the eyes.[53] In the Eastern Orthodox tradition, for instance, icons of biblical scenes and saints are understood as not merely images but as means of drawing us beyond our own space and time into the heavenly realm.[54] Even aside from iconography, there is no doubt that placing beautiful photographs and art depicting God's creation throughout our classrooms and our curriculum can help our students to think about beauty through a lens that is different from that of the surrounding culture.

Touch

Finally, Chrysostom introduces us to a fifth gate, the *gate of touch*. In his brief treatment of this gate, Chrysostom points out that it is unlike the others insofar as it "extends through the whole body," and while "it appears to be closed, yet it is, as it were, open and sends within whatever comes" ("Vain.," §63). As with his comments on the senses of smell and sight, Chrysostom's analysis of the sense of touch singles out the problem of luxury and comfort; as he says, "We are raising an athlete, let us concentrate our thought on that.

52. D. Smith et al., *Digital Life Together*, 143.

53. See D. Smith and Felch, *Teaching and Christian Imagination*, 89–105. See also Littlejohn and Evans, *Wisdom and Eloquence*, 66–67.

54. See Louth, *Introducing Eastern Orthodox Theology*, 113–21.

And so let him not use soft couches or raiment" ("Vain.," §63). The athletic metaphor points back to Chrysostom's call to "raise up an athlete for Christ" earlier in the homily ("Vain.," §19), again reminding us that Chrysostom understands education to involve consistent, perhaps even painful, exercise to form the student into a person of virtue. The New Testament itself makes frequent use of the image of an athlete disciplining his body to illuminate the nature of the Christian life. As Paul explains, "Every athlete exercises self-control in all things. They do it to receive a perishable wreath, but we an imperishable" (1 Cor 9:25).[55] The emphasis on self-control in this context leads naturally into a call for the asceticism that is the antidote to vainglory; just as an athlete must deny herself certain foods and discipline the body to maximize her athletic potential, so too there are bodily pleasures and luxuries that the Christian should deny in order to tame the cravings of the flesh and maximize the person's spiritual potential.

To turn to potential applications concerning this fifth and final gate, we need to remember that Chrysostom's commitment to the ascetical life reflects a time when asceticism was an increasingly common reaction to the perceived "softness" of imperial Christianity. If there is any concept from the early church more foreign to our lived experience of twenty-first-century North American Christianity, it surely must be the call to ascesis. To the extent that our society in general is driven by the desire to maximize pleasure and minimize discomfort, and to the extent that Christianity itself has been infected by the aforementioned moralistic therapeutic deism, the call to deny oneself as a practice of discipleship is all but vacant from our spiritual landscape.[56] And yet, recognizing that our students are growing up in an increasingly post-Christian society, this call to ascesis is perhaps especially relevant: if our students cannot learn to gladly, voluntarily choose to suffer for God, how can we expect them to take up their crosses when holding onto their Christian faith might cost them their friends, reputation, and careers? As Rod Dreher explains, "To rediscover Christian asceticism is urgent for believers who want to train their hearts, and the hearts of their children, to resist the hedonism and consumerism at the core or our contemporary culture. And it is necessary to teach us in our bones how God uses suffering to purify us for His purposes."[57] Asceticism, then, serves as

55. See also 2 Tim 2:5, 4:7; Heb 12:1.

56. On the more general relevance of this aspect of monastic spirituality for today, see again J. Smith, *Desiring the Kingdom*, 209: "A Christian community that seeks to be a cultural force precisely by being a living example of a new humanity will have to consider *abstaining* from participation in some cultural practices that others consider normal" (italics in original).

57. Dreher, *Benedict Option*, 64. See also Peterson, *Under the Unpredictable Plant*, 90.

a primary means of training for the spiritual life as we are formed into disciples who willingly walk with our Lord in the way of the cross.

For those of us who teach in settings where students have a superabundance of material comforts, what would it look like for them, as the next generation of Christ followers, to lean into the ancient Christian disciplines of ascesis as a countercultural form of incarnating the gospel and as a means of building moral and spiritual self-discipline? How would we even begin inculcating such an approach to the Christian life, when it is often utterly foreign not only to our students but to ourselves as well? Perhaps one very simple place to start, drawing on Chrysostom's picture of our students as embodied learners, is to engage students with learning that involves real labor—getting their hands dirty, if you will. Even something as simple as planting and tending a vegetable garden, the students and teachers together sweating in the heat and getting some mud on their clothes as they are tilling the earth, watering the seeds, and pulling weeds, can pull us out of our disembodied, virtual worlds to experience how our physical bodies interact with God's created world.[58] These embodied practices could then be connected to parts of the church calendar where it may be appropriate for students to consider engaging with some practices that are more ascetical in nature. Staying with our example of the vegetable garden, during Lent we could collectively take one day a week where we eat only the produce of that garden. Among the many profitable spiritual lessons that can be drawn from this activity are the importance of patience and perseverance (Gal 6:9), the nature of abiding in Christ and growing in him (John 15:5), and the goodness of enjoying the natural food that God has brought forth from the earth (Ps 104:14). There are undoubtedly complications that would need to be considered before carrying out this particular example, such as how such a practice might impact students from low-income families or who participate in after-school athletics, but this is no different from the challenges involved in planning any other kind of learning experience. Further creative thinking in this direction could generate additional learning experiences that challenge students to learn through the sense of touch and even contribute to their spiritual formation through ascetical practices. For further consideration of how we could invite students into this way of life, though, we need to consider the conclusion of Chrysostom's homily and his articulation of the ultimate goal of education.

In sum, Chrysostom's development of each of these sensory gates underscores the importance of recognizing that students are fully embodied

---

58. On manual labor, see Waal, *Seeking God*, 106–7. The attractions of such an approach are seen in the increased popularity of the outdoor-education movement; see further Louv, *Last Child in Woods*.

learners whose formation takes place across a wide array of sensory inputs. This is, of course, simply an extension of good pedagogy in general, as has been recognized by many Christian educators.[59] It is, moreover, how liturgical worship works.[60] It is precisely because of the importance of sensory inputs in creating lasting learning that we, following Chrysostom, must be so intentional about guarding these various gates, which we can summarize in the table below with some key questions for Christian educators to reflect upon:

Speech	Hearing	Smell	Sight	Touch
How am I training my students' habits of speech?	What kinds of stories are my students being exposed to?	What "scent" am I giving off to my students?	What visual stimuli are my students taking in?	How are my students practicing self-denial?
Am I inviting students to hold me accountable for my own speech?	Am I selecting age-appropriate resources for my students?	What "scent" are my students giving off to me and to one another?	How is the use of technology affecting my students' formation?	Are my students engaged in physical, embodied labor?

To reiterate, the work of "guarding the gates" of a student's soul cannot be the task of any one Christian educator. Rather, youth ministry experts suggest that Christian faith is most likely to "stick" with a youth when he or she has meaningful spiritual connections with at least five different Christian adults.[61] We cannot take on the pressure of being responsible for the entirety of a student's spiritual formation, nor should we. If we sense that we are the only adult Christian influence in a student's life, it is perhaps one of our most pressing duties to connect that student to other Christian adults who have the potential to further encourage them in the faith, be they fellow educators, youth pastors, or other members of the community. When our efforts are just one part of a broader team pouring into an individual student's life, our intentional efforts at spiritual formation in the classroom are more likely to bear long-term fruit in the life of the student.

Finally, it is worth noting that although Chrysostom's focus is very much on a defensive posture of "guarding" these gates, we can also (as I have tried to suggest in the examples above) view our role in more positive terms, thinking about how we can engage students' senses with that which is good, true, and beautiful. In other words, Chrysostom's cautionary words about

59. See, e.g., Littlejohn and Evans, *Wisdom and Eloquence*, 168.

60. See Bullis, "Applying St. Cyril's Pedagogy," 369.

61. See Powell and Clark, *Sticky Faith*, 101.

the senses need not exclude our deliberate attempts to cultivate students' appetites for the joy and wonder of God's creation.

GOVERNING THE CITY OF THE SOUL

Having described the role of the king (teacher) in guarding the gates (senses) of the city (student), Chrysostom concludes the homily with two primary laws that will contribute to the student's education and ultimate flourishing in faith and virtue.[62] While these laws generally either repeat or extend the points Chrysostom has made earlier in the homily, our brief attention to some of their major applications will help to reinforce Chrysostom's approach to educating students who are in fact embodied beings with a natural bent towards vainglory and sin but are capable of being formed, through education, into Christ's likeness.

The Law of Non-Defensiveness

First, Chrysostom urges that students learn to *defend others but not themselves.* As he summarizes his first law, Chrysostom argues that the child must learn "never to defend himself when ill used or suffering misfortune, and never to allow another to undergo this" ("Vain.," §69). While Chrysostom goes on to unpack this through illustrations that often reflect the patriarchal context of the ancient world in ways that are difficult to translate into the present day,[63] the clear spirit behind his instructions seems to be the dominical command to not resist an evildoer but to love one's own enemies (Matt 5:38–47), which is often a skill first learned (or not!) in the context of one's own sibling and peer relationships. Chrysostom's exposition first acknowledges the occasional need for active intervention on behalf of those who are suffering.[64] Indeed, in a school context, students may need to be challenged to not mind their own business when they see their peers being bullied but to work actively to stop such behaviors and create the kind of school community that would honor the Lord. Beyond this point, Chrysostom then places most of his emphasis on the child not being himself the

---

62. Chrysostom, "Vain.," §64: "Come now, when we have entered this city, let us write down and ordain laws, seeing that our arrangement of the gates is so fair."

63. For example, Chrysostom exhorts children to practice patience when they are slighted or disobeyed by slaves ("Vain.," §67). For an exploration of Chrysostom's rhetoric regarding slavery, see De Wet, *Preaching Bondage.*

64. Here Chrysostom cites the example of Moses striking down the Egyptian ("Vain.," §69; cf. Exod 2:11–12).

cause of suffering in another through attitudes of arrogance or entitlement. The goal in all of this is that the child cultivates gentleness, dispenses with anger, and treats people of all stations with kindness and brotherly love. Rather than demand that others serve at his beck and call, the child should learn to do things like wash his feet and draw a bath himself, for these things "will make him strong and simple and courteous" ("Vain.," §70).

In pursuit of this same goal, Christian educators have the opportunity through their mediation of conflict among students to pursue restorative justice by encouraging and affirming those students striving towards a posture of non-defensiveness and an outcome of reconciliation, while pushing back against students' natural inclinations towards self-preservation and score-settling. As Chrysostom himself indicates, the most powerful means of teaching this particular (and very difficult) virtue is that the parent or teacher "discipline himself" in this way "so as not to spoil the example that he sets" ("Vain.," §70). How do we handle and resolve conflict among our colleagues? What are our students, consciously or otherwise, learning about how Christians treat one another from their observation of our own behavior? Are we truly acting as servant-leaders who genuinely and consistently seek to put others ahead of ourselves and do tasks that might seem beneath us?

The Law of Self-Restraint

Second, Chrysostom demands that students learn to *exercise self-restraint, especially with respect to sexual desire.* For Chrysostom, the awakening of sexual desire in youths is nothing less than a wild, ravenous beast that places their souls in grave danger.[65] What is needed, he explains, is the aforementioned program of abstention and asceticism, such that students be kept from the theater and other places where arousal might take place and instead identify substitute forms of entertainment that would be neutral or perhaps even positive for the student's formation.[66] With particular insight, Chrysostom advises that if a student is nevertheless eager to go to the

65. With rather amusing matter-of-factness, Chrysostom informs us that "the medical guild tell[s] us that this desire attacks with violence after the fifteenth year" ("Vain.," §76). Some things, it appears, never change.

66. Chrysostom's special attention to the problem of sexual sin seems to reflect the significant attention this particular issue receives in the New Testament. As Paul, for instance, instructs the Corinthians, "Flee from sexual immorality. Every other sin a person commits is outside the body, but the sexually immoral person sins against his own body" (1 Cor 6:18). For a further discussion of why a right understanding of human sexuality is so central to the Christian faith in today's context, see Dreher, *Benedict Option,* 195–217.

theater, "point out any of his companions who are holding back from this, so that he may be held fast in the grip of emulation" ("Vain.," §77). As we all know, peer pressure cuts both ways, and when we have opportunities to connect students under our guidance with peers or friend groups that might be a positive influence, we should make the most of those openings. Besides this, Chrysostom returns to basic monastic disciplines as an antidote to the problem of lust. In particular, he singles out fasting and prayer as uniquely formational practices: "Let the boy be trained to pray with much contrition and to keep vigils as much as he is able, and let the stamp of a saintly man be impressed on the boy in every way" ("Vain.," §80). As indicated above, utilizing the church year as a means of inviting students to participate with us on the journey through Advent or Lent allows us to offer them a trial period to begin engaging in what might feel like unusual or difficult spiritual disciplines. Ultimately, though, Chrysostom identifies the attainment of wisdom as the chief antidote to lust.[67] Wisdom is, in fact, "the master principle which keeps everything under control" by grounding the soul in the "fear of the Lord" ("Vain.," §85; cf. Prov. 1:7). As Chrysostom concludes, "The fear of God and the power of forming such a judgment of human affairs as it behooves us to have are sufficient for wisdom. The summit of wisdom is refusal to be excited at childish things. So let him be taught to think nothing of wealth or worldly reputation or power or death or the present life on earth. So will he be sagacious" ("Vain.," §87). This, then, is Chrysostom's understanding of the *telos* of Christian education: the students' formation into Christ-likeness, as characterized by the fear of the Lord and the possession of wisdom, and as cultivated through ascetical practices.

As teachers, it is not enough, therefore, to simply instruct students to avoid immorality. Rather, we must present them with an alternative vision of the good life, one that is so compelling that their desire to live into that reality is greater than their desire for earthly pleasures. Chrysostom's emphasis on the fear of the Lord provides an important corrective to prevailing presentations of the Christian life in certain evangelical contexts, which at times can reduce God to little more than a self-help coach or needy girlfriend rather than the all-powerful Lord of the universe.[68] While we want to ensure

67. Chrysostom also has a lot of positive things to say about the benefits of arranged marriages ("Vain.," §81–82), but given that this is not much of an option in our cultural context, I have simply skipped over this point.

68. There are, of course, pockets of evangelicalism that may retain more of a fundamentalist, legalistic approach to God and the Christian life, and certainly the abuses of the "purity culture" of a previous generation have not helped in this regard, but I maintain that moralistic therapeutic deism is likely the more pressing context for most Christian educators reading this book.

that students understand God's amazing grace and boundless love, this does not mean that they should not also learn to "fear him who can destroy both soul and body in hell" (Matt 10:28). Cultivating a deeper appreciation for God's holiness and transcendence is, therefore, an essential part of training students in self-restraint. Alongside teaching students to obey the law of non-defensiveness and doing the intentional work of "guarding the gates" of the soul, we are well on our way to fulfilling Chrysostom's charge "to please God by rearing such athletes for Him, that we and our children may light on the blessings that are promised to them that love Him" ("Vain.," §90; cf. 1 Cor 2:9).

In drawing this chapter to a close, it is worth pausing again to note that in the final accounting it is the *relationship* between teacher and student that is at the core of our vocation. If a teacher does not have these kinds of authentic relationships with his students, empowered by his own hidden life with God, the other formative elements that will be discussed in the following chapters will not have the power and effectiveness that they would have in the context of such relationships.[69] Our attempts to "govern" the "cities" before us, to help our students turn away from vainglory and hedonism and instead become people of self-control, prayer, and wisdom, must therefore always be grounded in not just the *what* or the *how* of teaching but above all in the *who* of teacher and student. Above all, we must remember that, as Mark Yaconelli puts it, "what youth need most are people who know how to be present to God and present to others."[70] Our students long to be known, to connect with trusted adults with whom they can be vulnerable, authentic, and transparent. They are often looking not for advice, theological information, or special programming but simply for genuine and meaningful relationships. We may not be able to fully understand the world of our students, but we need not spend our years fruitlessly and exhaustingly chasing relevance and hipness! Rather, when we are ourselves deeply nourished in God's presence, we can incarnate an open, non-anxious presence to our students that will actually enable us "to get out of the center, to let God do the ministering, and to help youth notice and name God's presence in their daily lives"; just as Jesus "trusted that his presence—his prayers, words, silences, and acts of love—would be enough," so can we.[71] By being open to both God and our students in this

69. The same principle, it seems to me, is at work in our understanding of the church's worship and how it leads to mission; cf. J. Smith, *Desiring the Kingdom*, 169.

70. Yaconelli, *Contemplative Youth Ministry*, 24.

71. Yaconelli, *Contemplative Youth Ministry*, 59–60. See also Vanderstelt, *Gospel Fluency*, 25–35.

way, we can trust that the other aspects of our educational process will find fertile soil as we work to lead them on the path of spiritual formation.

THE STUDENT, REIMAGINED

In this chapter, through a close reading of John Chrysostom's homily "On Vainglory," we have reimagined the nature of our students through the lens of learners as complex, embodied persons who learn about virtue and vice through the senses. Given the weakness of our learners on account of the corrupting effects of sin, their greatest need is not simply information about God but rather a personal encounter with God. To the extent that we are responsible for shepherding our students' souls, our ultimate pedagogical aim must be nothing less than pointing them to another way of life, one characterized by faith, hope, and love, grounded in the same practices of contemplative spirituality that energize our own lives with Christ. While the primary way in which we do this is through our personal example and witness, empowered by our own rootedness in Christ and the power of the Holy Spirit, Chrysostom helps us to see that *what* we teach and *how* we teach can be just as significant in regards to the spiritual formation of our students. We are thus positioned to leave aside these more theological discussions on the nature of teachers and students and shift into a deeper analysis of the more "practical" aspects of teaching and learning, beginning with a further investigation into the formative potential of the curriculum itself.

This ch. was less about who R students R & more about what we need to do to train them —
        incuding specifics to the 5 senses
                Ultimate point

direct them away from their sinful inclinations towards others + heaven minded thinking

4

What Are We Teaching?

Basil of Caesarea and Training in Virtue

Having reimagined the identities of both teachers and students in light of patristic insights on the nature of spiritual formation, we arrive at a discussion of where conversations about Christian teaching and learning often begin: curriculum.[1] Educators have long recognized that all curriculum is essentially formative; whether it aims at producing good citizens, skilled laborers, or self-actualized consumers, curriculum always proceeds from an established worldview and points to some external vision of "the good life." Given, then, that all curriculum is designed in accordance with some kind of greater purpose or *telos*, a truly Christian one must be centered on a redeemed vision of the good life focused on Christ and the advancement of his kingdom.[2] What, though, does this look like in practice—not just for a Bible class but for English, history, and foreign language, or even math and science? While leaving aside questions about *how* course content is taught for the next chapter of this book, we will here focus on how the church fathers can give us insight into the way in which curriculum can inculcate Christian virtue in our students and train them accordingly, serving as a

---

1. Throughout this chapter, "curriculum" refers primarily to the academic content or body of knowledge taught in a classroom, with special attention to the selection of written texts.

2. See again J. Smith, *Desiring the Kingdom*, 26, 34, and the discussion in the first chapter of this book.

catalyst for growth into Christ's likeness. To guide our discussion, we will consider one of the most influential early Christian articulations of the relationship between Christian education and the curriculum of classical antiquity, Basil of Caesarea's "Address to Young Men, on How They Might Derive Benefit from Greek Literature."

Basil of Caesarea (ca. 330–79) is probably best known for his many contributions to Christian theological discourse in the second half of the fourth century. Basil's writings on trinitarian theology were instrumental in helping to resolve the Arian controversy about the nature of Christ, offering a vigorous defense of Nicene theology and paving the way for its triumph at the Council of Constantinople in 381, just two years after his death.[3] Basil is also celebrated for his works on asceticism and monasticism; his life and ministry, which were deeply informed by these perspectives, would pave the way for later ascetical bishops in his mold such as John Chrysostom and Gregory the Great.[4] As Basil's thoughts on the ascetical life matured, he came to organize one of the first monastic communities in the Greek-speaking world, earning him the title of Father of Eastern Monasticism.[5] As with the other church fathers examined in this book, Basil's asceticism serves as an important background theme for rightly interpreting his work, and we will engage with it throughout this chapter.

Most relevantly for this book, Basil provides us with a new lens for considering the formational impact of *what* we teach in the classroom. Over the course of the fourth century, church leaders such as Basil wrestled with the place of traditional pagan literature within Christian education. On the one hand, Christian scholars would come to identify the Scriptures as an alternative body of literature that could serve as the foundation for a more distinctively Christian education, even as the basic exegetical and rhetorical practices of the Greco-Roman schools were adapted for the new context.[6] On the other, though, familiarity with the classics of Greek literature was such a long-ingrained part of classical education that it was difficult to conceive of dispensing with them all together. Even John Chrysostom, who

---

3. On Basil's trinitarian theology, see further Hildebrand, *Trinitarian Theology*, 30–101. To briefly summarize the issue at stake, the followers of Arius maintained that there was a time when the Son "was not"; i.e., the Son was a creature and not coeternal with the Father. The orthodox response, as summarized in the Nicene Creed, was that the Son is uncreated and coeternal with the Father, "true God from true God." For an accessible summary, see González, *Story of Christianity*, 1:181–92.

4. On Basil's life, see further Hildebrand, *Basil of Caesarea*, 3–19.

5. On Basil's contributions to monastic theology and practice, see Hildebrand, *Basil of Caesarea*, 8–9, 12–13, 36–43.

6. See Young, *Biblical Exegesis*, 76.

as we saw in the previous chapter of this book seemed to suggest setting aside pagan literature in its entirety in favor of an exclusive focus on the Scriptures, nevertheless drew extensively on his own classical education in rhetoric for both his style and content.[7] It was, however, Chrysostom's younger contemporary, Basil of Cacsarea, who in his "Address to Young Men" would most famously and influentially articulate a mediating view on the role of pagan literature that might be as close to what would come to be the consensus position on the issue as we can find in early Christianity.[8]

To set this text in its proper context, it helps to understand the specific political and cultural forces that shifted this issue from being a largely theoretical discussion about education to one that in fact had profound real-world consequences. In 362, the pagan emperor Julian (known to history as "the Apostate"), determined to stop the rising influence of Christianity on Roman society and restore paganism as the religion of the empire, issued an edict banning Christians from teaching classical literature, costing Christian teachers their jobs at traditional schools of rhetoric and denying Christians the ability to make use of the pagan classics for apologetic purposes.[9] While Julian's program of religious reformation came to a quick end with his abrupt death the following year, his reign illustrates how continued tensions between Christianity and paganism were often centered on matters of education, which should not be surprising, given the classical world's universally agreed-upon understanding of education as essentially formative in nature.

Although we do not know the precise date or audience of Basil's address, it is nevertheless this broader context in which we can locate this discourse that appears to be directed at both students and teachers alike.[10] Given that debates about the compatibility of Christianity with secular philosophy and other non-Christian perspectives have scarcely abated in our present day,[11] Basil's ideas remain a relevant source for reimagining how we think about the curriculum component of Christian teaching and learning. In this chapter, we will begin by unpacking some of Basil's core assumptions

7. See Laistner, *Christianity and Pagan Culture*, 52–54. On early Christianity's relationship to classical *paideia*, see further Holder, "Saint Basil the Great," 395–98.

8. See Laistner, *Christianity and Pagan Culture*, 52; Deferrari, "Prefatory Note."

9. On Julian the Apostate's religious policy, see further Young, *Biblical Exegesis*, 70–75; González, *Story of Christianity*, 1:196–97.

10. See Hildebrand, *Trinitarian Theology*, 3–5. Holder identifies the students in view as grammar school students, likely between the ages of twelve and fifteen, though he notes that the wider audience likely included a wider range of Christian teachers and parents (Holder, "Saint Basil the Great," 400–401).

11. See Hildebrand, *Trinitarian Theology*, 6.

regarding education as they pertain to human knowledge of truth, then proceed to examine how Basil practically approaches curricular concerns in light of these presuppositions, and finally consider how curriculum can function as a training program for a life of virtue. As a result of our study of Basil's proposals, we will be better able to articulate a fresh vision of how inculcating Christian virtues through our curriculum can contribute to a student's formation into a disciple of Christ.

FOUNDATIONAL ASSUMPTIONS ABOUT TRUTH

While at the outset of his address Basil sets out in summary form the argument that he will develop over the course of this work,[12] he nevertheless quickly pivots to set out some initial philosophical presuppositions that motivate his approach to appropriating classical Greek literature for Christian education. For Basil, the need to accommodate truth for young learners and the real (albeit incomplete) existence of truth in the literature of pagan antiquity were non-negotiable elements of his understanding of education. We too will therefore begin with an examination of these foundational assumptions before turning to the main thrust of Basil's argument.

Accommodating Truth

Basil's first significant presupposition about teaching and learning is that students who lack maturity will need true knowledge not watered down or ignored but *accommodated* to their present capacity for understanding; that is, the truth must be presented as personally meaningful for and relevant to the unique needs of the learners. To establish the pedagogical context for this instruction, Basil first sets up a contrast between things temporal and things eternal. Echoing the Johannine perspective that "the world is passing away along with its desires, but whoever does the will of God abides forever" (1 John 2:17), Basil describes how earthly status and privilege will fade away even as "our hopes lead us forward to a more distant time, and everything we do is by way of preparation for the other life" ("YM," §2).[13]

---

12. Basil's ("YM," §1) initial exhortation to his audience is "that you should not surrender to these men [that is, the authors of the pagan classics] once for all the rudders of your mind, as if of a ship, and follow them whithersoever they lead; rather, accepting from them only that which is useful, you should know that which ought to be overlooked."

13. All quotations from the "Address to Young Men" are taken from the translation of Deferrari and McGuire.

The implication, Basil continues, is that our focus should be on those things that will contribute to the life to come. Therefore, we should let go of our pursuit of those things that will ultimately prove to be of no eternal worth.[14] The difficulty, though, is that having this kind of otherworldly focus is especially challenging for young people who lack the maturity to comprehend the glories of the life to come as they are presented in the Scriptures, or who have cognitive recognition of these truths but are uncertain of how to apply them or are fearful of their implications. As a result, Basil argues, they need analogies that can serve as "a preliminary training to the eye of the soul" and pave the way for later instruction in the mysteries of the Christian faith: "Therefore, just as dyers first prepare by certain treatments whatever material is to receive the dye, and then apply the colour, whether it be purple or some other hue, so we also in the same manner must first, if the glory of the good is to abide with us indelible for all time, be instructed by these outside means, and then shall understand the sacred and mystical teachings; and like those who have become accustomed to seeing the reflection of the sun in water, so we shall then direct our eyes to the light itself" ("YM," §2). In effect, Basil is claiming that there may in fact be more accessible, relevant footholds for initially accessing truth than the Scriptures themselves, which can be more daunting for students to interpret correctly and apply in meaningful ways to their lives.

The ability to adapt one's teaching to one's audience was a major emphasis of classical rhetorical training.[15] The church fathers extended this principle to God himself, whom they describe as adapting his revelation to human limitations.[16] In the same way, then, Christian teachers of late antiquity such as Basil recognized that some aspects of Christian theology are more readily accessible and capable of being comprehended than others and that some truths must be mastered before moving on to others. We see this with Paul, for instance, who in his preaching to the pagans of Lystra pointed them towards belief in the one creator God as a necessary first step before they would, presumably eventually, be able to receive the fullness of the gospel (Acts 14:15–17).[17] Following the same pattern, in the early church it was the norm for unbaptized catechumens to be dismissed prior

14. As summarized by Holder: "Whatever serves as preparation for the soul's eternal life with God is useful; whatever contributes only to the earthly life of the body is not" (Holder, "Saint Basil the Great," 403).

15. See Rylaarsdam, *John Chrysostom*, 18.

16. See Rylaarsdam, *John Chrysostom*, 22–30.

17. See also Paul's description of the Corinthians as "infants in Christ," whom he reminds that "I fed you with milk, not solid food, for you were not ready for it" (1 Cor 3:1–2).

to the celebration of the Eucharist, lest this mysterious sacrament be misunderstood.[18] Along the same lines, then, the mysteries of life after death and the eternal state can, if not grounded in a robust Christian anthropology, give way to profound misunderstandings, as evidenced by contemporary popular "Christian" belief in a heavenly, disembodied afterlife that is far more Platonic than it is Christian.[19] For his part, Basil was perhaps more concerned that the immature might conceive of the afterlife in an overly materialist form, as characteristic of the chiliasm popular among some Christians of his time.[20] In any event, given this understanding of the need to accommodate one's teaching to the capabilities and maturity of one's audience, Basil suggests a process of preparation, in which students receive "a preliminary training" for "the eye of the soul" so that they are prepared for "the greatest of all contests," the Christian life of progression toward God ("YM," §2). Basil will go on to argue that it is the pagan literature of classical antiquity that will serve this role of training young people for their eventual induction into the sacred mysteries of the Scriptures.

What Basil is helping us to see is that teachers have a responsibility to rightly accommodate their teaching to the intellectual, emotional, and spiritual levels of their students, just as God has accommodated himself to our human limitations. Through this framework, then, we will consider how accommodating to the academic and spiritual levels of our learners will include choices not only about curriculum but also about pedagogy and the process of faith formation, topics which we will explore in subsequent chapters. In so doing, we will not only better reach our learners but also have the privilege of emulating God's own pedagogy.

Finding Truth

Having argued about the need for accommodation, Basil arrives at his second foundational principle regarding truth in this address: that truth is found in *both* the Bible and the pagan literature of classical antiquity. In preparation for the study of the Bible, Basil suggests that students "must associate with poets and writers of prose and orators and with all men from

18. See, e.g., the account of Justin Martyr (ca. 100–165), *1 Apol.* 66.

19. On this subject, see Wright, *Surprised by Hope*, 13–27. Historic Christian teaching, on the other hand, has always stressed the hope of the resurrection of the body rather than the so-called intermediate state.

20. Chiliasm refers to the belief that Jesus will one day have a literal one-thousand-year reign on the earth with his saints. On debates over eschatology in the early church, see C. Hill, *Regnum Caelorum*.

whom there is any prospect of benefit with reference to the care of our soul" ("YM," §2). As Basil goes on to explain, just as a tree, which has the purpose of producing fruit, is additionally clothed with beautiful leaves, so the soul, which has the purpose of producing a life lived in conformity with biblical truth, may in fact also be adorned with the wisdom of pagan literature. There are, in other words, two purposes for this outside wisdom just as there are for leaves on a tree: protection of the truth and beauty in its own right ("YM," §3). Thus, pagan literature not only serves to prepare the soul to receive the mysteries of Scripture, but it also has value and meaning in its own right; even secular writings, therefore, can contain what is beautiful, good, and true (Phil 4:8).

To justify this perhaps surprisingly positive view of classical Greek literature, Basil appeals to the examples of Moses, who excelled in the wisdom of the Egyptians (Acts 7:22), and Daniel, who mastered the learning of *examples* the Babylonians (Dan 1:4). In both cases, Basil argues, these Old Testament saints proceeded from their mastery of secular learning to the contemplation of God and his "divine teachings" ("YM," §3). Thus, while in the previous chapter of this book we found that John Chrysostom had strong reservations about the use of pagan literature in the education of young people, *???* Basil confidently states that the literature of classical antiquity can in fact be useful for the soul. For Basil, pagan writings are clearly viewed as inferior to those of the Christians, and yet they nevertheless need not be viewed as the enemies of Christian formation.[21] This tension, in which Greek literature is viewed as both a genuine fount of truth as well as a clearly inferior and at times problematic source for a child's education, will lead to Basil's further treatment of the subject in the next section of his address.

Basil's reference to "beautiful" fruit also alerts us to his appreciation for what in the surrounding culture is not simply true but also characterized by beauty and goodness. Expanding our horizons beyond literature, we can easily see how our study of beautiful art and music created by human beings over the centuries, the diverse flora and fauna of our world, and even the transcendent poetry of mathematics can, by their inherent beauty and goodness, cultivate our students' appetites for the God who is himself the ultimate source and expression of truth, beauty, and goodness. Pointing our students to what is objectively good and beautiful in a postmodern world that prizes individual subjectivity is, admittedly, a countercultural task, and yet exposing students to these things, even from a very early age, is one

Bible is obviously superior text but other lit is useful & beneficial

---

21. See Holder, "Saint Basil the Great," 403. Laistner refers to Basil's conclusion as "the normal and, given the changing conditions of the times, the reasonable approach to the problem" of how Christians should engage with the pagan educational system and its literature (Laistner, *Christianity and Pagan Culture*, 51–52).

important way we can contribute to their spiritual formation.[22] As Robert Littlejohn and Charles Evans explain, "Students cannot be forced to accept the existence of absolute values, but as teachers, we ought to constantly push them to confront the question and to engage one another and the great wealth of ideas we expose them to as if these things really matter."[23] This, of course, requires that we as teachers cultivate our own appetites for what is good, beautiful, and true.[24] What, then, is objectively good and beautiful about the subject matter that you teach? How does your curriculum point students to things that are eternal? How can you help your students begin to appreciate those things that will lift their eyes beyond themselves and the vulgarities of much of our present culture to the things of God?

In sum, this presupposition encourages Christian educators to proceed with their work from the conviction that all truth is God's truth.[25] Whereas Chrysostom emphasized guarding students from the negative influences of the world, Basil here takes a more positive view, insisting that we have every reason to expect to find profitable uses for many secular writers and ideas, even as he will go on to provide some cautionary words of his own.[26] The most famous articulation of this point is surely that of Augustine of Hippo, who proclaimed that "every good and true Christian should understand that wherever he may find truth, it is his Lord's."[27] This notion of "plundering the Egyptians," of taking and converting for Christian use the best elements of pagan thought, thus came to be as influential in the West as it was in the East.[28] In approaching our curriculum, we should indeed make choices that point our students to what is good, beautiful, and true. Often it is the case that discussions about curriculum conclude with this point. Basil, however, offers us an opportunity to deepen our approach by appealing to further spiritually formative possibilities of curriculum, helping us acquire a vision for how our students can go beyond simply recognizing and appreciating what is good, beautiful, and true to growing in virtue. It is, in fact, this language of virtue that will come to dominate the rest of Basil's address and to which we now turn.

22. See Littlejohn and Evans, *Wisdom and Eloquence*, 26–27.

23. Littlejohn and Evans, *Wisdom and Eloquence*, 154.

24. See Littlejohn and Evans, *Wisdom and Eloquence*, 155.

25. On this subject, see further Gaebelein, *Pattern of God's Truth*, 19–35.

26. This is also, of course, a central implication of the Christian doctrine of common grace; for a conventional treatment of this doctrine, see Grudem, *Systematic Theology*, 657–65.

27. Augustine, *On Christian Doctrine*, 2.18.28.

28. See Augustine, *On Christian Doctrine*, 2.40.60.

INCULCATING THE VIRTUES

In the central portion of this address, having suggested that pagan learning has a place in the education of Christians, Basil sets out a framework for how Christians might appropriate the classics of Greek literature, encompassing the writings of the poets, historians, and orators. For Basil, provided that teachers (and eventually students themselves) have the ability to discern the formative value of pagan texts, the use of these writings can be justified insofar as teachers can draw on them to invite students to a life of virtue and provide them with examples of virtuous deeds while proceeding carefully regarding those portions of them that are unsuitable for maturing Christians.

Stopping the Ears

Basil begins this central section with a warning, focusing on the potential negative effects of students' exposure to pagan literature. As Chrysostom will later develop with reference to the "gate of the ear," Basil emphasizes the formative effects of words.[29] To this end, Basil insists with regards to the writings of the poets that "you ought not to give your attention to all they write without exception," on the principle that "familiarity with evil words is, as it were, a road leading to evil deeds" ("YM," §4).[30] Not only does Basil argue against carelessly exposing students to poems promoting polytheism or celebrating characters whose conduct is immoral or scandalous, but he goes so far as to claim that poems in which the protagonists pursue a worldview with a *telos* contrary to the pursuit of Christian formation, such as hedonism, must be treated with caution lest students' appetites for such a lifestyle be stirred.[31] Thus, Basil tells his students that "when they treat of wicked men, you ought to avoid such imitation, stopping your ears no less than Odysseus did, according to what those same poets say, when he avoided the songs of the Sirens" ("YM," §4). One may wonder, then, why Greek literature should not be abandoned altogether. As he will develop in the following stage of his argument, Basil nevertheless maintains that these writings do contain elements worthy of study and emulation. Pagan literature,

29. See again Chrysostom, "Vain.," §36–53.

30. Basil's reference to the student's soul needing to "be watched over with all vigilance" ("YM," §4) likewise anticipates Chrysostom's development of the teacher as the king or guardian of the child's soul; cf. Chrysostom, "Vain.," §23.

31. It appears that Basil is not suggesting avoiding such texts altogether but rather passing over those portions that prove problematic; cf. the discussion in Holder, "Saint Basil the Great," 404n26.

Basil concludes, must be treated akin to how bees approach flowers, "tak-ing only so much of them as is suitable for their work" and "suffer[ing] the rest to go untouched"; likewise, drawing a further comparison to nature, "just as in plucking the blooms from a rose-bed we avoid the thorns, so also in garnering from such writings whatever is useful, let us guard ourselves against what is harmful" ("YM," §4). The idea here is that of "custody of the eyes," the monastic notion which Arthur Holder explains as the recognition that while we cannot control everything that is placed before us, "at least to some degree we can choose what things we want to dwell upon and what things we will admire and love."[32] With this warning in place, Basil is now prepared to spell out more clearly what he finds "suitable" and "useful" from the writings of the Greeks.

Before we continue our analysis of Basil's argument, though, reflec-tions on this first general point are in order. In combination with Basil's reasoning concerning accommodation, his warning regarding pagan lit-erature can be instructive for modern Christian educators. While it is no doubt the case that our youngest learners should focus on positive examples and not be exposed to immoral or scandalous writings even in passing,[33] older students, and especially those in college or preparing to attend college, can benefit from guided engagement with such material, as appropriate to their higher levels of maturity and engagement with the world and in line with the aforementioned idea of "custody of the eyes." To this end, educators can help train students to recognize the formative pressures laying siege to them from every side. Indeed, if our students are to recognize that they are in a spiritual battle in which the enemy wants to redirect their hearts, through their habits and practices, away from God, we need to first train them, through intentional work in the classroom, to recognize and chal-lenge counter-formational "liturgies" in the world around them.[34]

The first step, though, is that as teachers we need to expand our own imaginations for what counter-formational messages we might inadvertent-ly be sending through our curriculum. In their book *The Gift of the Stranger*, David Smith and Barbara Carvill describe how foreign language textbooks "often focus more on the needs of the visiting tourist than on the world of the stranger," such that the vocabulary selected and the scenes portrayed

---

32. Holder, "Saint Basil the Great," 414.

33. For exposing young children to positive examples within church history itself, I cannot recommend enough Carey Wallace's inspiring *Stories of the Saints*, which fea-tures beautiful illustrations by Nick Thornborrow.

34. See again J. Smith, *Desiring the Kingdom*, 89–129, in which Smith invites us to exegete various secular "liturgies" in order to discern how and why they function to shape our desires in light of a particular understanding of human flourishing.

focus almost exclusively on enabling the student to be able to satisfy their needs for consumption and entertainment to the exclusion of engaging with local people or history in in any meaningful way.[35] Likewise, these textbooks tend to deliberately ignore religious themes in foreign cultures; the underlying assumption seems to be, then, "that faith and spirituality are relevant only to our own Christian subculture but are not woven into the fabric of life in the target culture."[36] Smith and Carvill go on to develop an approach to foreign language curriculum that intentionally seeks to cultivate in students a posture of curiosity, humility, and respect for the target culture, again demonstrating that the choices teachers make about curriculum, even at the level of textbooks and the kinds of exercises included therein, have profound implications for our students' formation.

Having so trained ourselves, we are then in position to help our own students recognize and challenge these counter-formational liturgies. Our students will benefit immensely from developing a critical eye and the ability to discern the messages being sent by various aspects of modern life and then evaluate them in light of the truths of Christianity.[37] Enabling our students to identify the view of human flourishing or vision of the good life undergirding various elements of the curriculum is, perhaps, an underappreciated approach to virtue formation in the classroom. While we will consider specific examples of this approach later in this chapter, it is simply worth noting that, in response to Basil's concerns about the deformative potential of some non-Christian writings, they might nevertheless be strategically used to help train students to recognize the false worldviews embedded in the world around them.

The Invitation to Virtue

With this warning in place, Basil in the next section of his address takes up the positive aspects of pagan literature, insisting that students can profit from "those passages of theirs in which they have praised virtue or condemned vice" ("YM," §4). In other words, one justification for the use of pagan literature is that it can act as an *invitation to virtue*. As we will see below, while Basil is careful to recast virtue (and, conversely, vice) according to the Christian gospel, it is nevertheless his contention that Christian virtues have some meaningful points of connection with classical ones. Taking Aristotle as a representative example, classical antiquity understood virtues to

---

35. D. Smith and Carvill, *Gift of the Stranger*, 128.

36. D. Smith and Carvill, *Gift of the Stranger*, 131.

37. See Holder, "Saint Basil the Great," 412.

encompass habits of right action, inclusive of attributes such as temperance, justice, fortitude, and prudence—attributes which would in fact become the four cardinal virtues of Christianity.[38] Thus, the classical literature of antiquity, insofar as it promotes virtues that align with the teachings of the Bible, should be set before students in order to form their souls: "For it is no small advantage that a certain intimacy and familiarity with virtue should be engendered in the souls of the young, seeing that the lessons learned by such are likely, in the nature of the case, to be indelible, having been deeply impressed in them by reason of the tenderness of their souls" ("YM," §5). Training in virtue is difficult, Basil acknowledges, and yet the virtuous life will ultimately be one that is smooth, beautiful, and pleasant. After all, he explains, unlike any earthly possessions, virtue cannot be stolen away by others and will endure into the next life.

By the nature of the examples from classical literature to which he appeals, Basil indicates that the texts he has in mind are not so much abstract, philosophical treatises on the nature of the good. Rather, as was the case with poetry, it is those stories or narratives that celebrate the concept of virtue that are to be placed before students. In fact, as Alasdair MacIntyre observes, in the classical world "the chief means of moral education is the telling of stories."[39] It is the stories that we teach our students, then, that have the power to incline their souls towards either virtue or vice. Anticipating his next point, Basil emphasizes the notion that virtuous actions are the desired outcome of this kind of education; it is not enough, he explains, simply to hear these stories and keep them at arm's length. Instead, having absorbed these stories, we "try to show forth their words in our lives" ("YM," §6). Precisely because training in virtue does not end with intellectual instruction, simply presenting the stories themselves without a call to action is insufficient.[40] Like Gregory, therefore, Basil is intensely concerned with the alignment of words and actions, and his next point will in fact expand upon the relationship between the stories of classical literature and virtuous actions in more detail.

38. For overview, see bk 2 of Aristotle's *Nicomachean Ethics*; for discussion of these virtues and others, see bks 3–5. See further MacIntyre, *After Virtue*, 146–64.

39. MacIntyre, *After Virtue*, 121. This is, of course, also true of Jesus and other Jewish rabbis from the ancient world who primarily taught through stories or parables. Today, businesses and organizations continue to recognize that stories can be a compelling means of providing inspiration for people to buy their products or become members of their groups; cf. Heath and Heath, *Made to Stick*, 204–37.

40. See Holder, "Saint Basil the Great," 406: "The teaching of these pagan writers about virtue are not only to be repeated and admired; they must also be put into practice in the students' lives."

What Basil and MacIntyre both help us to see is the power of story for stirring our souls to pursue something good, beautiful, and true beyond ourselves. Many of our most powerful cultural phenomena tap into our deepest desires to live lives of purpose, meaning, and adventure. We can easily imagine ourselves as *Star Wars*' Luke Skywalker, gazing up at the twin suns of Tatooine, yearning to explore the larger galaxy, or as *The Lord of the Rings*' Frodo Baggins, unexpectedly receiving the One Ring from Gandalf and having to contemplate a dangerous journey from the Shire to Mordor. We connect powerfully with the very human struggles and redemption arcs of characters such as *Les Miserables*' Jean Valjean or *The Brothers Karamazov*'s Dmitri Karamazov. Such stories resonate so powerfully in our culture precisely because there seems to be in all of us a longing for a call to adventure that will enable us to take our first steps into a larger world, to plunge us into a battle between good and evil that transcends our otherwise seemingly mundane existence and challenges us to embrace our best, most virtuous selves.[41] Thus, while in our context it is the movies of the Marvel Cinematic Universe and not the epic poems of Homer (the Marvel movies of the ancient world) that are most likely to fire our students' imagination for lives of virtue and meaning, the underlying principle is the same: to the extent that these stories inspire our students to a life of virtue and meaning, we as Christian educators need not wholly reject every aspect of culture around us but can identify within it accessible starting points for conversations about virtue and meaning. As Holder contends, we can affirm what is good in our culture because "God was not left without a witness in the ancient world (Acts 14:17), nor is any modern culture utterly cut off from the signs of God's active presence."[42] And we can, time and again, point our students back to God's story of creating, redeeming, and restoring our world as the most true and beautiful story of them all, a story within which we are invited to find our ultimate identity and purpose.

In comparison with Basil's circumstances, however, we have to face the additional challenge of living in a society that has increasingly lost sight of any agreed-upon notion of virtue or vice. Rather, we live under the scourge of emotivism, which MacIntyre defines as "the doctrine that all evaluative judgments and more specifically all moral judgments are *nothing but* expressions of preference, expressions of attitude or feeling, insofar as they are moral or evaluative in character."[43] As opposed to societies of the past,

---

41. On the "monomyth" or "hero's journey" underlying these and many other legends, myths, and stories, see the classic work of Joseph Campbell, *Hero with a Thousand Faces*.

42. Holder, "Saint Basil the Great," 413.

43. MacIntyre, *After Virtue*, 11–12 (italics in original).

in our present day we can no longer appeal to shared notions of virtue and vice as objective realities that exist outside of ourselves. Undoubtedly influenced by the triumph of postmodernism and moral relativism, the "heroes" portrayed in our popular culture are in fact better characterized as "anti-heroes"; traditional, earnest protagonists are passé, while we instead celebrate the moral reprehensibility of protagonists such as *Breaking Bad*'s drug-dealing murderer Walter White. As MacIntyre explains, "without an overriding conception of the *telos* of a whole human life, conceived as a unity, our conception of certain individual virtues has to remain partial and incomplete."[44] At the societal level, we should not therefore be surprised to see that virtue, in fact, becomes vice, and vice becomes virtue. This is a real challenge, but, as we will see, Basil can help expand our imaginations for how Christian educators can use their curriculum to promote virtue in their students.

The Deeds of Virtue

Closing this central section of his address, Basil identifies the educator's task of inviting students to the life of virtue as inseparable from the work of exhorting them to virtuous actions. "And since the virtuous deeds," Basil explains, "of the men of old have been preserved for us, either through an unbroken oral tradition or through being preserved in the words of poets or writers of prose, let us not fail to derive advantage from this source also" ("YM," §7). Thus, Basil articulates a second, albeit closely related to the first, justification for the use of pagan literature: to give students *virtuous deeds to emulate*. Here he is clearly echoing his earlier point about providing students with positive role models from pagan literature, but he does so now with a greater degree of specificity by focusing in on the specific examples of virtuous deeds recounted in these texts.

The particular examples Basil selects, along with his means of interpreting them for a Christian context, reveal much about his understanding of how Christians can utilize pagan literature. While Basil draws his examples from pagan authors, he defines the virtues in light of Jesus's teaching in the Sermon on the Mount.[45] Thus, for instance, Basil suggests that Socrates's willingness to let a drunk man repeatedly strike him without resistance or

---

44. MacIntyre, *After Virtue*, 202; see also Holder, "Saint Basil the Great," 412.

45. See Holder, "Saint Basil the Great," 406. As Holder goes on to explain, "Basil has provided nothing less than a Christian reinterpretation of the Greek ideal of virtue, while urging his young audience to read profane literature with a sanctified imagination informed by the admonitions of holy scripture" (Holder, "Saint Basil the Great," 407).

physical retaliation is akin to Jesus's teachings not to resist an evildoer and to turn the other cheek (Matt 5:38–42). The appeal of such examples, Basil argues, is that such positive examples can be "recalled to memory" by the student in pivotal moments of decision-making, "for whoever has been instructed in these examples beforehand cannot after that distrust those precepts as utterly impossible to obey" ("YM," §7). Such positive role models thus empower students to make virtuous choices in their own lives.

In this way, Basil points to a Christian solution to MacIntyre's point concerning the loss of a shared notion of virtue in our contemporary society. After all, Christians *do* have a unified, comprehensive understanding of the ultimate purpose of human life.[46] It is precisely because the Christian way of discipleship provides a fully-orbed vision of the good life that it can generate a concomitant set of virtues whose exercise leads to attaining that particular *telos*.[47] In light of this, we should not be surprised to find both similarities and differences between Christian and pagan virtues, and it is precisely where these two intersect that Basil identifies pagan literature as useful for pointing to the same virtues in the Scriptures.[48] To bring this into the modern day, we might consider how even the popular music that our students listen to can function similarly to how pagan literature did in Basil's times. One colleague, for instance, regularly plays songs for his classes as a way into discussions about the good life. Rush's 1982 song "Subdivisions," for example, lends itself to a conversation about how teens often feel stifled and force-fed a life script by various adults, peers, and society at large. How tragic it is, he agrees, when the hopes and dreams of youth get stifled or stamped out in order simply to have a safe, well-paying job. Of course, the counterculture that Rush has in mind is doubtlessly different from the alternative path of the cross, but Rush correctly intuits how God has planted in our hearts a desire to live for something much greater than ourselves and a lifestyle of consumerism and materialism.[49]

Basil, then, helps us to see that we can continue to find in the culture around us aspects of God's truth in ways that are easily relatable and

46. See MacIntyre, *After Virtue*, 202.

47. See MacIntyre, *After Virtue*, 184. Besides the four cardinal virtues noted above, the Christian tradition has also recognized the three "theological" virtues of faith, hope, and love.

48. For Christians such as Basil, then, *aretē* comes to be redefined around notions of "excellence, truth, goodness, and obedience to God's commands" (Holder, "Saint Basil the Great," 405n28).

49. More contemporary examples of this same theme may be seen, for instance, in songs such as "Stressed Out" by Twenty One Pilots and "Suit and Tie" by Judah and the Lion.

accessible for our students. Beyond this, as we have indicated above, with older students we can additionally use those places where the values of this world do not align with those of the Christian faith to push them towards understanding and then embracing Christian virtue. Several illustrations show how this approach can work in practice.

Starting with one of my own history classes, in my lesson on the effects of industrialization on Gilded Age America, I task students with reading and analyzing texts by Andrew Carnegie and Russell Conwell, who each in his own way sought to justify the extreme levels of economic inequality resulting from industrialization.[50] In his 1889 essay "The Gospel of Wealth," Carnegie, the famous steel magnate and philanthropist, drew on the ideas of social Darwinism to argue that the widening gap between rich and poor was actually a positive thing. Carnegie suggests, directly against the historic Christian practice of almsgiving, that the rich should help only those who are willing to help themselves. Carnegie's articulation of his vision of the good life, depending as it does on the application of Darwin's ideas of the "survival of the fittest" to human society—and all the racist and utilitarian implications embedded in that late-nineteenth-century approach—is designed to cause my students to stop and question if this is in fact "gospel," as Carnegie puts it. Likewise, in his famous 1890 lecture "Acres of Diamonds," Baptist minister Russell Conwell makes explicit his contention that God wants us to get rich; given that the poor are being punished by God for their sins, we should help only those who are truly deserving. With his nauseatingly self-congratulatory dialogue and exaggerated language, Conwell's vision of the good life, centered on consumerism and materialism, is unmistakable and offensive to my students. In reality, though, this *telos* is hardly different from that of modern society, and this sets it up nicely for further interrogation with my students, as will be detailed below. After all, I probe, does human flourishing not consist of going to the best college, getting a marketable degree, making a lot of money, and enjoying all the comforts of this world (while giving back to the truly needy only out of one's "surplus")? After having had students ascertain the view of human flourishing undergirding the approach to wealth found in Gilded Age America, I then have my students identify what the Bible and even the broader Christian tradition have to say about the subject.[51] Beginning with the account of Jesus

50. Carnegie, "Gospel of Wealth," and Conwell, "Acres of Diamonds." For overview, in the context of the broader prosperity gospel movement in the United States, see Bowler, *Blessed*, 31–32.

51. Of course, the Bible (much less the Christian tradition) may not always speak univocally or clearly on some particular issues, but this in turn provides a window into equipping students to read Scripture well, priming them in the basics of biblical

and the rich young ruler (Mark 10:17–22 pars.), we find that Jesus never promises material wealth as a reward for obedience and that Jesus is very clear that costly economic stewardship is an essential aspect of Christian discipleship, as it demonstrates that the believer's true master is God and not Mammon (Matt 6:24). Contra Carnegie and Conwell, Christians must be sacrificially generous and not proud, refusing to lord their wealth over the poor or claim moral superiority over them. Likewise, as students read portions of Basil's powerful homily "To the Rich," which features a sharp yet beautiful call to economic justice, they are challenged to reflect on their own attitudes towards money.[52] While not losing sight of differences in historical context and interpretive challenges, this activity nevertheless provides an opportunity to challenge students' natural inclinations as Americans towards materialism and consumerism. Basil himself serves as a powerful example of virtuous living in this regard; after his baptism, Basil sold some of the inheritance he had received and distributed the proceeds to the poor.[53]

For a second example, a colleague teaching eighth-grade English uses George Orwell's book *Animal Farm* to engage students in conversations regarding ways in which they are being influenced without even knowing it. Orwell's critique of Soviet-style totalitarianism and propaganda is extended into the students' own world through discussions about how advertising and social media aim at influencing the attitude of a community toward some cause or position and why people sometimes do not respond or act out even when they know something is wrong. These forms of influence, students discover, are purposefully designed to target the insecurities of young people, who generally lack sufficient confidence in their own identity and the critical discernment necessary to understand and resist these forms of manipulation. Many students, in fact, may actively aspire to become "influencers" who wield precisely this form of power over others. As the study of *Animal Farm* progresses, students are challenged to consider how their study of this text might illuminate Paul's charge, "Do not be conformed to this world, but be transformed by the renewal of your mind, that by testing you may discern what is the will of God, what is good and acceptable

---

hermeneutics, which is itself a worthy topic to work through with them. This is certainly the case with respect to a passage such as Mark 10:21; though Christ's command is directed at this particular man and thus likely not a universal demand for all would-be disciples, we must balance that fact out with Jesus's strong statements in Mark 10:23–25, which must in turn be balanced out by the Lord's teaching in Mark 10:27!

52. For an accessible translation of Basil's homily "To the Rich," see the excellent Popular Patristics volume *On Social Justice*, in which C. Paul Schroeder pulls together several Basilian homilies on this theme.

53. See Schroeder, "Introduction," 19.

and perfect" (Rom 12:2). The Christian virtue of wise discernment, then, is set up in contrast with our natural inclinations to have our opinions blown about by every external influence, whether for good or for ill.[54]

It is not just in the humanities that teachers can use their curriculum to invite students to a life of virtue. The sciences, for instance, raise a host of moral issues that can be engaged from a Christian perspective. For instance, new innovations in areas such as fertility science and genetic engineering, as well as emerging conversations around the subject of transhumanism, raise important questions about human personhood and if there should be limits to how we should apply scientific knowledge. Likewise, the subject of creation care has become an increasingly important focus for many Christians eager to reframe human beings' relationship with the created world in a way that better takes into account the full sweep of the Christian story of creation, fall, redemption, and consummation.[55] Virtues such as humility and temperance can, therefore, be cultivated alongside the study of science. In a society that continues to experience rapid technological change, it will be exceedingly important to train Christians who will be able to engage these difficult topics from the perspective of biblical truth.

What, though, about mathematics, ostensibly the most difficult subject to integrate with Christian faith? As a colleague who teaches math points out to his students, math is in fact a means by which we can come to a better understanding and appreciation of the Creator and his created order, for math is a language used to describe the universe and its systematic order.[56] Consequently, he emphasizes that while mathematics develops many practical skills needed for numerous vocations, it is nevertheless also the case that the study of mathematics cultivates a deeper understanding of God's creation and clearly manifests goodness, truth, and beauty.[57] A recognition that all wisdom and knowledge is found in Christ (Col 2:3) is, after all, the starting (and ending) point for a Christ-centered perspective on mathematics. For instance, geometry highlights the relationship between the intuitive and rational aspects of truth. In the same way that a geometric system begins with fundamental postulates that cannot be proven, a Christian worldview rests on foundational faith presuppositions that remain beyond the reach

54. For further discussion of integrating faith and the teaching of literature, see Gaebelein, *Pattern of God's Truth*, 64–69.

55. See, e.g., Moo and Moo, *Creation Care*.

56. For what follows, he draws especially on Gaebelein, *Pattern of God's Truth*, 57–64.

57. It would not be an exaggeration, perhaps, to suggest that doing math is itself an act of worship: if a major feature of Christian worship is speaking God's words back to him, and math is one way in which the language of God is embedded into creation, our engagement with math is a form of engagement with God's "second book."

of reason. Likewise, calculus reveals that the infinite may help us better understand the finite. Full understanding of the infinite is not possible or required for it to have a relationship with or an effect on the finite. Just as we do not have to count to infinity before applying this concept to the study of a limit, so we do not need to prove God's existence before we believe. Beyond these connections between the study of mathematics and principles of the Christian faith, so also our study of math can exhort students to virtuous actions. Statistics, for example, cultivates a deeper understanding of God's creation by providing a conceptual framework and practical tools for sound judgment and wise decision-making.[58] David Smith shares the example of a mathematics textbook that includes a unit on trigonometric functions, logarithmic scales, and quadratics. All of these topics are examined through the lens of studying the 2004 Indian Ocean tsunami, with students reflecting on how these principles of mathematics relate to relevant issues such as modeling a wave or dropping relief supplies from aircraft. As Smith summarizes, "Alongside the mathematical practice, students are invited to reflect on a Christian response to suffering, natural disasters, and global inequality."[59] Students with an inclination or passion for math are thereby exhorted to consider how expertise in even the most abstract fields of mathematics could be used to serve the kingdom of God. Thus, as this section has demonstrated, the invitation to the pursuit of virtue can serve as a unifying theme across all subject matters, providing an overarching framework for developing curriculum in such a way that all roads lead to Christ.

LIVING THE VIRTUES

In the above section, we found that Basil justified the selective study of Greek literature on the basis that it can help invite students to a life of virtue and provide them with examples of virtuous deeds. Now, in the final portion of his address, Basil makes an explicit call for students to be trained in these virtues so that they actually live them out.

For Basil, truth is not a mere set of philosophical abstractions but rather something to be received with a particular "end in view," by which Basil means the attainment of God's eternal "prizes" in the life to come ("YM," §8). Thus, just as an athlete trains for the competition or the musician practices for the recital, Basil suggests that Christians engage in a regimen of training and practice in virtue, lest they find themselves apart from God for

---

58. There appears to be a biblical connection between rightly using mathematics and justice; cf. Lev 19:35–36.

59. D. Smith, *On Christian Teaching*, 92.

eternity.[60] The underlying assumption, which is that students can be trained to develop habits that will enact virtue, is essentially Aristotelian.[61] Thus the role of the teacher is to provide such opportunities by which students can practice the virtuous life, such that choosing virtue becomes the default course of action for the student.

How, though, does a Christian go about this training? Unsurprisingly, Basil appeals to the practices of asceticism as the evidence that our increasing awareness of truth is shifting our gaze from earthly to eternal things. Thus, anticipating Chrysostom's articulation of the same theme a couple of decades later, Basil insists that purification of the soul "consists in scorning the pleasures that arise through the senses," commenting briefly on how the senses of sight, hearing, smell, touch, and taste can all be corrupted ("YM," §9).[62] If we are able to "despise the body," he continues, "we should be slow, methinks, to feel admiration for any other thing that man may possess" and can likewise avoid "living with a view to popularity and giving serious thought to the things esteemed by the multitude" ("YM," §9).[63] In particular, our embrace of God's truth is meant to lead us away from these things and instead toward the cultivation of those virtues that act as "travel-supplies" for the soul's journey to eternity ("YM," §10). It is in the cultivation of virtue, to which our knowledge of the truth points, that we may, as Paul puts it, run the race to receive the prize (1 Cor 9:24–25). While Basil's ascetical ideal might be a bit overly negative on our embodied nature insofar as he insists that the body should be "despised" ("YM," §9), his overall appeal to reject the hedonism characteristic of both his time and ours is an enduring message that we need to continue to hear.[64]

---

60. See Holder, "Saint Basil the Great," 407. The athletic metaphor for the Christian life should remind us of both Paul (1 Cor 9:24) and Chrysostom ("Vain.," §19, 39, 63, 68, 90).

61. See Aristotle, *Nicomachean Ethics*, 2.4.1. The existence of common grace suggests that even nonbelieving students can learn to live in a virtuous manner; cf. Grudem, *Systematic Theology*, 660. Proverbs, for instance, contains a great deal of wisdom that non-believers can profit from even apart from a saving knowledge of God in Christ.

62. See again Chrysostom's treatment of this theme in "Vain.," §28–63.

63. Throughout, Basil continues to draw on examples from Greek literature, suggesting that, as Holder puts it, "Basil has by no means lost sight of his original aim," insofar as he here "puts into practice the very method he has been recommending: Christian virtues are taught by examples from pagan literature" (Holder, "Saint Basil the Great," 408).

64. For a modern corrective to Basil on this point, see the recent interest in the "theology of the body" as popularized by figures such as Pope John Paul II. The implications of the eternal Son of God becoming incarnate as a human being in a real body could also be further explored at this point.

Helping our students to go beyond simply identifying the virtues and values of the kingdom of God to living in line with those things is, perhaps, one of our most pressing duties as Christian educators. Basil's insistence on asceticism might tempt us to disregard this goal altogether, but to return to one of Basil's initial presuppositions, we can take heart from the principle of accommodation. Given their present capacity for understanding and our current cultural context, our students are probably not going to resonate with a highly demanding call to asceticism as a form of Christian discipleship, and yet we still have the opportunity to introduce our students to ways of living out the Christian faith in deep, meaningful, and virtuous ways.[65] The Christian virtues that we want our students to exemplify, after all, are not solely for the purpose of their own spiritual growth but also exist to leaven our society as a whole.

As argued above, many of our students have little sense of Christian virtue and how that might translate into lived practices. How might we successfully accommodate such learners (and, perhaps, many teachers) who might struggle with knowing how to connect curriculum to discussions of Christian virtue? Moreover, how might we train our students in actually living out Christian virtue? My vision for how to approach these questions has been greatly informed by a model known as Teaching for Transformation, currently led by the Center for the Advancement of Christian Education at Dordt University. One component of this approach is the development of ten different "throughlines," grounded in the broader story of creation, fall, redemption, and consummation.[66] These throughlines, meant to be embedded across the full scope and sequence of a school's curriculum, are defined as "discipleship habits and practices that both form the learners and transform God's world around them." To this end, they aim to expand students' imagination for what it means to live as a disciple of Christ and call students to active engagement with the aspect of Christian identity or virtue embedded in that throughline.[67] To demonstrate how this approach works, I will briefly survey how my present institution has adapted this notion of throughlines to support its declared mission.

After setting forth a brief summary of our understanding of "the story" (that is, the biblical narrative according to historic Christian orthodoxy), we invite students to adopt this story as *their* story: to repent of their

---

65. See Littlejohn and Evans, *Wisdom and Eloquence*, 20.

66. On "creation-fall-redemption-consummation" as the framework for a Christian worldview, see Littlejohn and Evans, *Wisdom and Eloquence*, 47–49. On the gospel as the center of "the true story," see Packer and Parrett, *Grounded in the Gospel*, 82–83; Vanderstelt, *Gospel Fluency*, 49–63.

67. "Throughlines."

sins, acknowledge Jesus as King, and reorder their lives in accordance with their identity as citizens of the kingdom of God, living as the people of God for the sake of others.[68] With the help of the Holy Spirit, we pray, they will live out their part in this story by becoming more like Christ, embracing the values and virtues of the kingdom of God and experiencing spiritual transformation. Recognizing that it can be difficult, sometimes, to unpack precisely what all this means for our day-to-day lives, we offer a set of twelve throughlines, anchored in the biblical narrative and organized according to our school's mission statement, to help our community grasp some key aspects of what is entailed by Christian discipleship:

Our school exists to bolster Christian families in rearing young people who go on to college and life with . . .		
A passion for learning . . .	For others ahead of self . . .	And for the living and active Jesus.
Truth Finder	Justice Seeker	Image Bearer
Creation Explorer	Servant Leader	God Worshiper
Order Discoverer	Community Builder	Christ Emulator
Beauty Maker	Diversity Embracer	Spirit Possessor

A close analysis of one of these throughlines will suffice to demonstrate how this works in practice. As depicted in the table above, our school's mission statement declares that the school will cultivate in its students "a passion for others ahead of self," and to that end the school has identified four throughlines that unpack Christian virtues that we believe contribute to forming students who have this passion for others ahead of self. The one we will examine here, Diversity Embracer, grew out of another of our school's core values, which is that our students would experience diversity that reflects the body of Christ, seeking unity among different kinds of people and recognizing that God created all people in his image. In our current political and cultural climate, there are few conversations that have the lightning-rod potential of those touching on race, social justice, and diversity. To the extent that it is all too easy to ignore these issues or simply to capitulate to echoing what the world is saying about them, a carefully grounded biblical throughline has the positive potential to articulate and promote, in an accessible way, a shared diversity vision for unity in Christ. By identifying and developing a particular Christian virtue we want to inculcate in our students—in this case, that they would seek Christ-centered unity among

68. On finding our place in God's story, see Vanderstelt, *Gospel Fluency*, 64–205; Choung, *True Story*, 150–71.

different kinds of people—we can then build out a training program for building this virtue across our curriculum.

After providing a brief introductory overview that introduces the school community to the biblical and theological basis for this throughline,[69] we then list the desired student outcomes related to engaging as a Diversity Embracer, drawing upon a "think-feel-act" taxonomy that can be stream-lined into "heads-hearts-hands," which is represented in the table below:[70]

Students who are Diversity Embracers *will engage their*		
HEADS by noticing people who are different from them and recog-nizing them as image bearers.	HEARTS by growing in understanding and em-pathy for people who are different from them.	HANDS by engaging in loving, serving, and learning from people who are different from them.

To put this another way, this throughline communicates to our community that we are aiming to produce students who go on to college and to life with a passion for others ahead of self as expressed through the specific call to be Diversity Embracers. Given that the curriculum is the primary (though by no means exclusive) place in which these throughlines are em-bedded, we then offer curriculum connections to help teachers find ways, through their curriculum, to design learning experiences that would help students engage their identities as Diversity Embracers. As presented in the table below, the heads-hearts-hands taxonomy continues to drive the organization of the throughline and ensure that we reach not only students' minds but their affections and behaviors as well:

69. Some key biblical passages informing this throughline include Gen 1:27; Matt 28:18–20; Gal 3:27–28; Eph 2:14–18; 4:2–6; Phil 2:1–11; Rev 7:9–10.

70. This heads-hearts-hands approach will be discussed in more detail in ch. 6 below.

To help students become Diversity Embracers, *we could design learning experiences that would help students to engage their*		
HEADS by noticing people who are different from them and recognizing them as image bearers by . . .	HEARTS by growing in understanding and empathy for people who are different from them by . . .	HANDS by engaging in loving, serving, and learning from people who are different from them by . . .
Learning about people from other cultures and praying for their specific needs. Recognizing the contributions of female and/or non-majority people in our various fields of study. Including female and/or non-majority authors in our reading lists.	Showing how what we are learning could engage with issues that are significant to people who are geographically or culturally distinct from them.[71] Modeling a posture of humility and openness to people who are different from them. Inviting a diverse range of parents or outside guests to present or interact with our students. Having students engage in historical role-play to build empathy with those who are different from them.[72]	Connecting existing service projects, field trips, mission trips, and Jan.-term experiences to the idea of engaging with people who are different from us. Working in groups or teams that include a diverse array of people for the purpose of reaching a common goal. Designing assignments that would involve engaging with local people with whom they would otherwise not interact.

These examples are, of course, in no way meant to be prescriptive or exhaustive; rather, they simply reflect some strategies used by different teachers in our community to promote this virtue and help facilitate creative reflection in other teachers who engage with this throughline. By keeping these examples somewhat general, we hope to show that teachers across all divisions and subject areas could use this throughline in their curriculum. It helped

71. See D. Smith, *On Christian Teaching*, 91–92.

72. For example, one colleague who teaches US history teaches the Civil War and post-Civil War period through the lens of five American families (white Southerners, Northern industrialists, black sharecroppers, Nez Perce, and Chinese immigrants) in order to begin to understand the lived realities of these very different groups of Americans. In the next unit of his class, students actively role-play as the descendants of these families as they formulate an appropriate definition of "success," given their race, gender, legal status, and past family history, and then consider what pathways to success would be open to them, given those circumstances.

me see, for instance, that the curriculum for my tenth-grade Bible class did not include any African-American authors, leading me to bring in portions of Esau McCaulley's book *Reading While Black* as a way of introducing my students to the reality that Christianity is not an exclusively or even primarily "white man's religion" but rather a faith that has been deeply and authentically African from its beginning.[73]

To bring this back to Basil, and to his particular concern for the use of pagan literature by Christian educators, we can see how this approach could serve as a useful method for connecting non-Christian sources of learning to training in Christian virtue. If it is true, as I have suggested above, that we often struggle to identify Christian virtues in the first place, then these throughlines give a ready-made list of aspirational values to which we can connect what we are reading in English class or studying in the laboratory. To return to my example lesson on Gilded Age America, our exploration of matters of wealth and poverty could then be explicitly connected to the Justice Seeker throughline, which promotes the virtue of striving for justice among all people and respecting the dignity of every human being. Specifically, the format of the throughline provides me with a foundation upon which to build further learning experiences that would allow students to continue engaging this virtue with their heads, hearts, and hands. For instance, I could extend this lesson by inviting them to make a careful examination of their own spending habits and consider how their choices about how they spend their money may reveal the priorities or perhaps even idols in their lives. The next step, then, would be to exhort my students to think of concrete steps that they could take to grow in the area of financial stewardship by setting aside some portion of their allowance or earnings as alms for the poor, in whatever way the individual student feels led. In so doing, I am pushing my students to engage with this virtue with their hands and not just their heads; while our history lesson had as its primary focus the effects of industrialization on Gilded Age America, we ultimately arrived at a discussion of Christian virtue that has hopefully enlarged my students' understanding—not just of the Gilded Age but also of their responsibilities as disciples of Jesus Christ with respect to wealth and economic justice.

Likewise, in the aforementioned unit on *Animal Farm*, this teacher extends the lesson into the students' lived experience by calling them to join her in a two-week social media fast, exploring how social media might be serving the purpose of conforming their hearts and minds to the patterns of this world. This easily connects with the Truth Finder throughline, which promotes the virtue of pursuing sound learning, new discovery, and wisdom

73. See McCaulley, *Reading While Black*, 96–117.

in light of the recognition that God—and not the world—is the source of all truth. From this unit and other applications of the Truth Finder throughline elsewhere across the curriculum, students are challenged to find their true identities in Christ alone and, from that foundation, be better equipped to see the realities around them, discern the extent of their alignment with Christian truth, and act to resist evil, regardless of the cost.[74]

To address one possible objection to this approach: how does this work if many of our students are not regenerate or not walking on the path of discipleship? Just as Aristotle intuited that we learn virtue through practicing virtuous habits, these throughlines can provide even non-Christian students with opportunities to practice "trying on" some aspects of the Christian life in a non-threatening way, even as we pray that the Holy Spirit would thereby enable them to "taste and see that the Lord is good!" (Ps 34:8). Indeed, in inviting students to join with us on the journey of faith formation, we can proceed mindful of the reality that "everyone when he is fully trained will be like his teacher" (Luke 6:40). Moreover, given that God's common grace to all people entails that even nonbelievers can participate in what is good, beautiful, and true, we can trust that our non-Christian students of goodwill will be able to embrace many, if not all, elements of Christian virtue.[75] The throughlines described above generate just such a means of providing all students with opportunities to engage with the values and practices of the Christian faith for the ultimate purpose of inviting them fully into the way of life as virtuous disciples of Christ.

CURRICULUM, REIMAGINED

In this chapter, as we have walked through Basil of Caesarea's "Address to Young Men," we have sought to reimagine how curriculum can play a formative role with respect to promoting a life of virtue in our students. In line with the principle of accommodation and in light of the recognition that "all truth is God's truth," we can heartily embrace everything that is good, beautiful, and true from our surrounding culture as fit for a Christian education, especially as we employ it as a springboard for conversations regarding a life of Christian virtue. In order to move students forward on the path of discipleship, we have found that curriculum can function as a rigorous training program for growing students in virtue, pushing them beyond simple head knowledge of the values and virtues of the kingdom of God to a transformation of their emotions and behaviors. The concept

74. See Dreher, *Live Not by Lies*, 5.
75. See Littlejohn and Evans, *Wisdom and Eloquence*, 46.

of throughlines, rooted in God's story and aiming at specific curricular applications, provides just such an approach to training students in virtue. Of course, for such a training program to succeed, there must be attention paid not only to *what* is being taught but to *how* that curriculum is being taught. With this in mind, we turn to our next chapter and begin to unpack some elements of a distinctively Christian pedagogy.

5

How Are We Teaching?

Benedict of Nursia and Formative Practices

Having considered how Christian educators' attention to curriculum design can inculcate Christian virtue in students, we now turn our focus to the spiritually formative possibilities inherent in the actual teaching and learning process itself. While the literature on the integration of faith and learning has tended to emphasize what is being taught and the people who are doing the teaching, there is an increasing recognition among Christian educators that even our most mundane-seeming pedagogical choices are formative. As David Smith explains, "An account of Christian education that focuses only on the truth of what is taught, and fails to address the meanings molded through *how* it is taught and learned is at best incomplete."[1] In this chapter we will consider how our pedagogical choices—by which I mean what Smith describes as our "choices about how time and space are used, what interactions will take place, what rules and rhythms will govern them, what will be offered as nourishment and used to build shared imagination, and what patterns will be laid out for students to move among"[2]—can contribute to our students' spiritual formation into disciples of Christ. For the purposes of better grounding this emerging discussion in the riches of

---

1. D. Smith, *On Christian Teaching*, 4 (italics in original).
2. D. Smith, *On Christian Teaching*, 12.

historical theology, this chapter will engage with arguably the most famous and influential of all pieces of monastic literature, the *Rule* of St. Benedict.

Given his immense importance for the history of Western Christianity, surprisingly little is known about Benedict of Nursia (ca. 480–547). The only significant ancient source for reconstructing Benedict's life dates from near the end of the sixth century and is written by Gregory the Great. Found in the second book of his *Dialogues*, Gregory's account of Benedict's life purports to be drawn from the personal recollections of four of Benedict's disciples.[3] According to Gregory, Benedict was born into a privileged family and received a classical education in Rome, and yet at some point he rejected the path of worldly wisdom and success in order to pursue a life of solitude and prayer.[4] After living alone for three years in a cave outside of Rome,[5] Benedict went on to found a series of monastic communities, including the one at Monte Cassino where he would serve as abbot and live out his days.[6] In recounting the many miracles performed by Benedict throughout his life, Gregory—in line with his own pastoral concerns and theological agenda, no doubt—presents Benedict as a committed ascetic who nevertheless was willing to engage in the active life for the sake of others.[7]

While Gregory's portrait of Benedict focuses on him as an ascetic and miracle worker, history has primarily remembered Benedict for his contributions to the development of Western monasticism, as handed down in the form of the *Rule* that he wrote for his monks at Monte Cassino. While Benedict's *Rule*, likely written around 540, was hardly the first such monastic rule found in early Christianity, it gained influence across Europe after it was taken to Rome in the late sixth century, and from there to England, France, and the Holy Roman Empire over the following centuries.[8] As Christians from a variety of eras, denominations, and walks of life have discovered, the *Rule* is a master class in spiritual formation; many Christians who have never taken monastic vows have nevertheless realized that it contains what has been called "a proven strategy for living the Gospel in an intensely Christian

3. See Gregory the Great, *Dialogues*, 2.prol.

4. See Gregory the Great, *Dialogues*, 2.prol.

5. See Gregory the Great, *Dialogues*, 2.1.

6. See Gregory the Great, *Dialogues*, 2.4, 2.8.

7. See Demacopoulos, *Gregory the Great*, 29–30; White, "Introduction," ix–xi; cf. Gregory's argument in *PR*, 1.5. On the historical reliability of Gregory's account, see Waal, *Seeking God*, 16–17.

8. See further White, "Introduction," xiv–xxv. On the influence of the Benedictines on the English church and Anglicanism in particular, see Waal, *Seeking God*, 21–22; Thornton, *English Spirituality*, 76–83. Augustine of Canterbury, who was himself a Benedictine monk, became the first archbishop of Canterbury in 597.

way."[9] Over the course of its seventy-three chapters, Benedict's *Rule* sets out the rules, routines, and rhythms that will contribute to the formation of a community in which this gospel life can be pursued. With a keen attention to detail and a clear understanding of the human condition, Benedict delineates the path by which his monks, who would have taken vows of stability, fidelity to monastic life, and obedience (*RB*, §58), can "progress in this way of life and in faith," such that they "shall run on the path of God's commandments" until the day of their death (*RB*, prol.).[10] Central to this path is the cultivation of humility, which Benedict understands as the chief end by which we ascend the ladder to our heavenly home (*RB*, §7). It would not be an exaggeration, then, to say that the primary purpose of the monastic life according to Benedict is growth in humility; accordingly, we can best understand the many rules and rhythms of the *Rule* as working towards this ultimate *telos*.

How, though, can this ancient handbook on the monastic life inform our approach as Christian educators today? To the extent that the *Rule* casts a vision for establishing a "harmonious community" and provides a clear and comprehensive plan to foster such an environment and help each individual monk on his journey of spiritual formation,[11] Benedict's insights can likewise shape our thinking about how we can build a harmonious community in our own classrooms and assist each student in his or her spiritual formation. Building this bridge between the monastery and the classroom is further aided by Benedict's own admission that his monastic community could adequately be described as "a school for the Lord's service" (*RB*, prol.).[12] Not for nothing, then, has the *Rule* been viewed as "one of the favorite pedagogical manuals in the West."[13]

Thus, with the assistance of Benedict's *Rule*, in this chapter we will examine how the practices, rituals, and routines of the classroom have formative power. First, we will contemplate how Benedict's vision for community life and restorative discipline can inform our pedagogy and matters of classroom management. Then, we will consider Benedict's insights into how decisions about the use of time and space can contribute to our students'

---

9. Dreher, *Benedict Option*, 53.

10. All translations of the *Rule* are taken from *RB 1980*.

11. See White, "Introduction," vii.

12. This "education" that Benedict sought to provide his monks would surely meet James K. A. Smith's definition of the word (*Desiring the Kingdom*, 26): "a constellation of practices, rituals, and routines that inculcates a particular vision of the good life by inscribing or infusing that vision into the heart (the gut) by means of material, embodied practices."

13. Schütz, "To Serve Life," 154.

growth into Christ's likeness. Given the length and varied content of the *Rule*, we will address these items topically rather than walk through the text section by section, as is the procedure elsewhere in this book. Having engaged with these different themes of the *Rule*, we will be better able to understand how all aspects of our pedagogy can point our students to Christ and his kingdom.

FORMATIVE PRACTICES OF COMMUNITY LIFE AND DISCIPLINE

To use the evocative image of David Smith, if we want our classrooms to be "gardens of delight," places of spiritual nourishment and growth,[14] we must pay close attention to those practices that shape and sustain our learning communities. Mixing metaphors, in light of Parker Palmer's call for a classroom space that is both "hospitable and charged,"[15] we might envision each classroom as a garden that has places for rest and shelter but also contains surprises, delights, and challenges around every corner. It is with this vision in mind, then, that we consider how the *Rule* challenges us to think about the two pivotal subjects of community life and student discipline.

Community Life

The earliest Christians were known for the quality and intensity of their life together. Following Pentecost, Luke reports, the first believers "devoted themselves to the apostles' teaching and the fellowship, to the breaking of bread and to the prayers" (Acts 2:42); what is more, "all who believed were together and had all things in common" (Acts 2:44). Through church history, monastic movements can be understood as attempts to recreate this moment in the life of the early church. The particular innovation of Benedict's *Rule* was its emphasis on how the monks were to relate to one another in love.[16] This principle is reflected throughout the *Rule*; near its outset, for instance, in his commentary on the Great Commandment (Matt 22:37–39 pars.), Benedict reminds his monks, "Your way of acting should be different from the world's way; the love of Christ must come before all else. You are not to act in anger or nurse a grudge. Rid your heart of all deceit. Never give a hollow greeting of peace or turn away when someone needs your love" (*RB*, §4).

14. See D. Smith and Felch, *Teaching and Christian Imagination*, 89–138.
15. Palmer, *Courage to Teach*, 77–78.
16. See Waal, *Seeking God*, 18–19.

This is a community that will be characterized by a love that expresses itself through unhesitating obedience to superiors (*RB*, §5), restraint with respect to speech (*RB*, §6), and, especially, humility. Benedict in fact articulates a series of twelve steps by which the monks will cultivate this virtue and thereby ascend to the perfect love of God (*RB*, §7).[17] Moreover, the love within the community entails that everyone's needs will be met (*RB*, §34). The brothers continually serve one another, "for such service increases reward and fosters love" (*RB*, §35), with special concern that the sick receive extra honor and care (*RB*, §36). Benedict returns to the centrality of this mutual love at the conclusion of the *Rule*, noting that obedience must in fact be "shown by all, not only to the abbot but also to one another as brothers" (*RB*, §71), driven by a zeal that "each try to be the first to show respect to the other" (*RB*, §72; cf. Rom 12:10). With great clarity of vision, then, Benedict saw that the demands of the gospel must be worked out in community, in the real and messy human relationships that ultimately need not distract us from our pursuit of God but in fact enable us to progress on that journey as we learn to love our neighbors as ourselves.[18] This ability to cultivate a community of mutual support, empowerment, and edification must flow from a shared vision for the community that lifts each individual person out of concern for the self and into a larger mission to love God and love others.[19] Note well that creating such a community is a communal endeavor; "many 'partners' are involved here, and all bear responsibility in their own way, with no sharp distinction between active and passive roles."[20]

Benedict's *Rule* thus puts forth a vision for community life that can help us to reimagine the kind of learning community that we seek to cultivate in the classroom. There is, of course, a large gap between the classroom and the monastery; we do not, unless perhaps we work and live at a boarding school, live among our students over the course of many years. Our classroom community likely exists for only a few hours a week over the course of a semester or academic year; we have not pledged ourselves to one another and a common way of life until death. Nevertheless, our classrooms can be places where we invite students to experience elements of a Christian community, where we can pursue an alternate vision of the good life

17. On the Benedictine approach to humility, see further Chittister, *Wisdom Distilled*, 51–66.

18. See Chittister, *Wisdom Distilled*, 42. See also Dreher, *Benedict Option*, 67–71.

19. See Chittister, *Wisdom Distilled*, 44–47, 108–20; Schütz, "To Serve Life," 160. See also Waal, *Seeking God*, 116: "Endlessly the Rule makes room for each individual to grow in holiness at his or her own speed, in his or her own way. The Rule is devised for people, the community exists for the sake of the individual, and not vice versa."

20. Schütz, "To Serve Life," 157.

to what is found in the rest of the world and plant seeds that will hopefully bear fruit later in the course of their lives. To put it simply, if we desire to create a learning community that reflects these Benedictine values, we need to engage our students in the work of creating, cultivating, and committing to a shared way of life in pursuit of a shared purpose. Three brief examples will suffice to illuminate some of the ways in which we can intentionally cultivate this kind of classroom culture.

First, we can collaborate with our students to establish a shared vision for the culture of the classroom. While Benedict may not have worked with his monks in crafting the *Rule* itself, it was nevertheless the case that monks choosing to join a Benedictine monastery did so knowing precisely what was expected of them and what they could expect from others in the community.[21] Having joined the community, they worked together to live out the vision set forth in the *Rule*, keeping one another accountable to its principles. Along these same lines, one of my colleagues devotes the entirety of the first three days of his Latin classes each year to crafting a classroom covenant, aiming to create buy-in and ownership over the common culture in which teaching and learning will take place. On the first day, he begins by having his students reflect on selected verses from Scripture (e.g., Gen 1:27, 3:8; Eph 2:19–22), guiding them into an understanding of one another as image bearers, made by God to be creative, responsible, and relational beings. Then, on the second day, he assigns them to reflect on the school's mission, helping them identify growth in their relationship with God, growth in their relationships with others, and their use of their gifts to encourage one another as the ultimate objectives of the course beyond the Latin-specific learning standards. Finally, on the third day, he challenges them to put this all together by having them consider how they can go about creating a learning environment that reflects the above principles. Specifically, each student responds to four questions. *What do my classmates need from me? What do I need from my classmates? What do I need from the teacher? What does the teacher need from me?* As a result, students collectively set and commit to a class vision for a Christ-centered learning environment.[22] For example, one class declared its intention to be a community where "students and teachers will explore and observe creation, seek knowledge, honor and serve others as image bearers of the Creator God, and pursue excellence in their work, doing everything as unto the Lord." Specific expectations for student engagement followed from this intention, including such positively-framed

21. As the *Rule* indicates, a novice, who has not yet taken his vows, "should be clearly told all the hardships and difficulties that will lead him to God" (*RB*, §58).

22. Depending on the maturity level of the students, the actual work of articulating or crafting this vision may require more or less direction on the part of the teacher.

notions as "actively listening to others" and "serving and honoring others with your contributions to class."[23] While such a slow, intentional approach to building classroom culture may appear to some to be a "waste" of class time that could be devoted to learning content or skills, my colleague has found that this approach has created more student buy-in such that the resulting decrease in classroom management issues has, on the whole, provided a net gain of instructional time.[24]

Second, we can design learning experiences that empower individual students to build up one another in love. Just as Benedict called his monks to exhort, edify, and support one another, our classrooms can be places where students are called to put one another ahead of themselves. We can, for instance, aim to establish rhythms and routines in which our anxious and harried students can slow down and provide nourishment to one another. To take just one example, in my New Testament courses, we open each period with a brief student devotional. Over the course of the semester, we manage to walk through the entirety of the Sermon on the Mount (Matt 5–7). Jesus's teaching in the Sermon on the Mount is full of practical advice for how students can love one another better, such as by forgiving others when they are wronged by them (Matt 6:14–15), not judging others (Matt 7:1–5), and doing unto others what they would want done unto them (Matt 7:12). On the one hand, this assignment was designed to develop students' skills in line with the objectives of the course: students are graded on how well they research, interpret, and apply their assigned passage, as well as on their overall communication skills. On the other hand, though, I am really after something deeper: that these students would encourage and exhort one another, from their hearts, about what it might mean to live the life of the kingdom of God in their own time and place. My students are more open to being challenged to stop bullying others, gossiping over text messages, or engaging with pornography when it is one of their own peers (and not me as the teacher), who is vulnerable about these struggles and shares the desire to change. This same motivation drives Common Table, a student-led time of worship, prayer, and fellowship that takes place at my school early on Friday mornings. Because attendance is entirely voluntary, and because students have taken ownership of different aspects of the communal gathering,

23. This approach contrasts with one that appeals exclusively to students' self-interest by linking the rationale for following classroom rules to individual incentives such as grades or negative disciplinary consequences.

24. This should also remind us that there is no such thing as "wasted" time in the classroom, as learning is always happening even apart from formal instruction. See also the discussion of classroom culture in Littlejohn and Evans, *Wisdom and Eloquence*, 51–58.

students are much more poised to give and receive exhortations to faith and holiness within this community than they are in a formal, mandated chapel setting.[25] These opportunities provide students with chances to reorient one another to a way of life that honors both God and neighbor.

Third, we can forge unity amongst our students through the tasks to which we set them. Benedict required all his monks to share equally in the work of the community (*RB*, §35), which would have forged bonds among the monks regardless of the social status they had held prior to entering the monastery.[26] In this way, the brothers "should each try to be the first to show respect to the other" (*RB*, §72; cf. Rom 12:10). Like Benedict's monks, my students come from a range of socioeconomic, cultural, and educational backgrounds; what is more, each class can develop hierarchies based on who is the most intelligent or who has the most charismatic personality. Schoolwork has the possibility to foster and accentuate these differences, but it also has the potential to break them down. My school sets the tone in this regard with our seniors on a multi-night retreat before the start of the academic year. As much as they may complain about sleeping in cabins without air conditioning, sweltering in the relentless Georgia summer heat, or having to eat camp meals of questionable freshness and quality, these shared moments of suffering and bread-breaking powerfully strengthen the bonds within the senior class, as well as between students and their faculty advisors who share these living conditions.[27] Indeed, with respect to the actual work that we assign to students, we have the choice of designing activities, assignments, and assessments that isolate each individual student, promoting competition and the success of the self, or those that require students to cooperate with one another, promoting collaboration and the success of the team. What if, for instance, we tasked our highest-achieving students with assisting those who are most struggling? What if we viewed success in terms of helping everyone succeed?

Beautifully illustrating such an approach, a colleague who directs high school theater intentionally considers the role of understudies in her program. Rather than merely waiting in the wings in case a lead gets sick or injured, her productions' understudies actually perform the lead roles in

---

25. I suspect even something as small as exhorting students to greet one another when they pass in the hallways could be a revolutionary idea for some; as Chittister provocatively suggests, this community ritual may be less about saying hello than it is recognizing and acknowledging the presence of God in the other person (Chittister, *Wisdom Distilled*, 164).

26. See Waal, *Seeking God*, 118.

27. On the Benedictine understanding of the spiritual power of sharing meals together, see Chittister, *Wisdom Distilled*, 174–76.

half of the ticketed shows, with the leads first mentoring them and then performing the ensemble roles in their place. For the stars of the show, then, their success is tied not simply to their own success but to training the next generation of thespians to grow in their abilities too. She has found that this approach demonstrates to everyone that there are no unimportant roles both on the stage and off, unifying the cast as they cheer on each and every member of their team. Another colleague, who teaches middle school English, assigns students to groups that have an even mix of high, middle, and low achievers based on a pretest. These groups work together to complete practice assignments, worksheets, and activities throughout the unit. Then, they take the posttest individually, and if all students in the group have improved their grade, they all receive a bonus. This is designed to promote cooperation over competition, incentivizing all students to work towards the good of the group. Student feedback has been very positive, identifying this teamwork as playing a large role in facilitating their academic progress.[28]

In sum, our engagement with what the *Rule* says about community life can help us articulate to our students the importance of embracing an others-centered focus. In other words, as Christian educators, we aspire to teach not only academic content or skills but to create and participate in a learning community characterized by faith, hope, and love. Every student should be encouraged to make the most of his or her unique gifts and talents but always within the broader calling of serving one another in love. As Joan Chittister elaborates concerning Benedictine spirituality, "There is no question that my goal in life must be to develop the best in myself to the best of my ability. The question is, why? In Benedictine spirituality, the answer seems to be that we grow to full stature in life in order to carry someone else. Perhaps, in fact, we never grow to full stature until we have learned to carry someone else."[29] And then, Lord willing, we might truly experience a taste of that which leads the psalmist to exclaim "how good and pleasant it is when brothers dwell in unity!" (Ps 133:1). What, though, is the role of authority—and, by extension, discipline—in such a classroom community? To this subject we now turn.

Student Discipline

Human nature being what it is, this vision of community life can be realized only if there is a robust plan for responding to members of the community

28. This colleague notes that she has developed this idea based on the STAD approach of Robert E. Slavin.

29. Chittister, *Wisdom Distilled*, 120.

whose actions threaten to undermine the unity of the whole. Leaving the classroom aside for a moment, we find that the history of Christianity shows there to be twin dangers to be avoided when it comes to the subject of discipline within the church: on the one hand, a brittle legalism that stifles grace, and, on the other, a laissez-faire attitude in which discipline in effect ceases to exist. Christ himself, however, foresaw the need for genuine discipline within the church (Matt 18:15–20), while nevertheless exhorting believers to limitless forgiveness towards one another (Matt 18:21–35). Likewise, Paul insisted that notorious and unrepentant sinners be disciplined, both for the good of the sinner who needs to come to repentance and for preserving the integrity and holiness of the community itself (1 Cor 5:1–13).[30]

These principles were used to guide not only church life but also monastic communities. Benedictine spirituality contains a keen awareness that both individuals and the community as a whole benefit from discipline.[31] Indeed, in foregrounding his overall approach in the *Rule* Benedict calls for "a little strictness in order to amend faults and to safeguard love" (*RB*, prol.). Perhaps the central duty of the abbot is to discipline his monks, "always striving to cure their unhealthy ways" (*RB*, §2). Similarly, the primary duty of the monk is arguably obedience, which Benedict identifies as "the first step of humility" (*RB*, §5). For those monks who persist in disobedience, which is nothing less than a manifestation of the antithesis of the humble spirit that the *Rule* is so concerned to cultivate, the *Rule* outlines a series of measures, including private and public rebuke, corporal punishment, excommunication, and ultimately expulsion from the monastery (*RB*, §23–30). Benedict's pedagogical approach, then, is one in which "the failure, the weak, the difficult, the outsider, the stubborn all receive an unusually generous chance and period of grace in which to change."[32] Discipline, then, cannot be separated from love which intends the good of the other.

Moreover, Benedict's views concerning discipline ultimately stem from his recognition that a community is not, at the end of the day, a mere collection of isolated, atomized individuals; rather, each member of the community is accountable to one another because each impacts the well-being of the whole.[33] To return to perhaps the central theme of the *Rule*, the humility that is necessary for climbing the ladder of ascent to the heavens requires engaging with such principles as remaining steadfastly obedient even under difficult or unjust conditions, finding contentment in even the

---

30. See also the discussion of this theme in Heb 12:3–11.
31. See Waal, *Seeking God*, 130.
32. Schütz, "To Serve Life," 159.
33. See further Chittister, *Wisdom Distilled*, 133–46; Waal, *Seeking God*, 129–40.

most menial of work, and considering oneself the least of all the brothers (*RB*, §7). All of these, it would appear, are characterized by the humility that places the needs of the community ahead of one's own desires or preferences. Discipline, then, is the loving response of the abbot to the wayward monk whose selfishness is keeping him from the path of humility. Likewise, if we as Christian educators desire to create learning communities characterized by love, unity, and humility, we cannot shy away from the task of discipline within the context of our classrooms. Again, three brief examples will be sufficient to shed light on some of the most salient aspects of this point.

First, discipline is necessary to uphold the expectations we set for the classroom. To return to the example of my colleague's efforts to craft a classroom covenant with his Latin students, this process not only generates specific expectations for student engagement but also leads naturally into a clear explanation of the how and why of classroom discipline. Thus, he promises his students that he will honor them as individuals who uniquely bear God's image and that he will strive to share God's love with them. And it is precisely because of these things, then, that he promises that he will hold them accountable as valued members of their class community. The strength of this approach to discipline is that it is grounded in an explicit articulation of mutual respect in light of the recognition that each person in the classroom is an image bearer.[34] Rather than appearing arbitrary or punitive, discipline is presented in its rightful place as a measure that is undertaken for students' own good and as the means to restoring the kind of classroom community envisioned in the class's covenant, which was, after all, what the students themselves had crafted to reflect their own hopes and aspirations for learning. Indeed, the more that we can clearly connect common student actions that require disciplinary responses, such as plagiarism, to how these actions harm the well-being of the community as a whole, the more we can expect to see higher levels of student buy-in for maintaining these expectations. The mutuality inherent in this approach is also effective; as Littlejohn and Evans write, "Faculty who intentionally see themselves as partners with students in learning and growing provide themselves with a tremendous opportunity to form their students."[35] My colleague, as he has developed this approach over a number of years, has observed higher levels of student engagement with the course content and with one another, contributing to a learning environment that is increasingly gospel-centered and spiritually formative.

---

34. See Littlejohn and Evans, *Wisdom and Eloquence*, 55.

35. Littlejohn and Evans, *Wisdom and Eloquence*, 55. See also Gaebelein, *Pattern of God's Truth*, 91–93.

Second, discipline must work towards the common goal of sanctification while taking into consideration the unique social, spiritual, and emotional journey of each learner. On the one hand, because our goal for every one of our students is that they would be increasingly conformed into Christ's likeness, we know that discipline is a necessary means towards the end of our students' emotional, social, and spiritual growth. And yet, despite this common goal, the *Rule* recognizes that the abbot must, like Gregory the Great's spiritual director providing different medicines for different patients with varying illnesses and symptoms, "prune [the brothers' faults] away with prudence and love as he sees best for each individual" (*RB*, §64). For instance, a student who turns in an assignment late because of a family crisis should receive a different response from us than a student who turns in the same assignment late but has a history of not turning in work on time and spent the entirety of the previous evening playing video games. Thus, an individualized approach to discipline, seeking to take into account which treatment or pruning might best accomplish the goal of a student's growth and maturity, is a key insight on discipline that we can take from Benedict's *Rule*.[36]

Third, we can help our students to develop habits of confession and repentance. These patterns are perhaps most profoundly illustrated in the *Rule* when Benedict urges, "If a monk is reproved in any way by his abbot or by one of his seniors, even for some very small matter, or if he gets the impression that one of his seniors is angry or disturbed with him, however slightly, he must, then and there without delay, cast himself on the ground at the other's feet to make satisfaction, and lie there until the disturbance is calmed by a blessing" (*RB*, §71). This emphasis on public shaming as a means of discipline, as also illustrated by the examples of the monk late to the divine office being forced to stand apart from the other monks for the remainder of the service (*RB*, §43) or the excommunicated monk prostrating himself at the oratory entrance until the abbot readmits him (*RB*, §44), is entirely at odds with the disciplinary ethos of almost all schools, including Christian ones—and for good reason! But without endorsing this specific approach, I believe that we can still learn from the *Rule's* insistence that spiritual and moral formation require learning to engage in habits of confession and repentance. As the *Rule* goes on to explain, "If someone commits a fault while at any work . . . he must at once come before the abbot and

---

36. See Littlejohn and Evans, *Wisdom and Eloquence*, 57: "The challenge, of course, is to ensure that disciplinary measures are just. We say 'just' and not 'fair' since fairness suggests equality and 'sameness' for all. Instead, discipline should 'fit the crime' for any given student in any given situation." Here I might add it should "fit" not only the crime but the student as well.

community and of his own accord admit his fault and make satisfaction. If it is made known through another, he is to be subjected to a more severe correction. When the cause of the sin lies hidden in his conscience, he is to reveal it only to the abbot or to one of the spiritual elders, who know how to heal their own wounds as well as those of others, without exposing them and making them public" (*RB*, §46).

The goal, then, is that Benedict's monks would confess their faults of their own volition, owning up to their mistakes and failures in order to receive the "healing" of their elders. The church has long recognized the need to train her people in the rhythms of confession and repentance; most liturgical forms of worship, for example, begin with the congregation devoutly kneeling to confess their sins before God.[37] Like David, we tell the Lord that "I know my transgressions, and my sin is ever before me" (Ps 51:3) and pray, "Create in me a clean heart, O God, and renew a right spirit within me" (Ps 51:10). Confession, writes Richard Foster, "is a means of healing and transforming the inner spirit."[38] This foundational rhythm of the Christian life is therefore something that we want to cultivate in our students, which is why some formal mechanism (such as an honor council) has the potential, if executed well, to be so important for helping students learn to own up to instances of sinful behaviors such as lying, cheating, and stealing. Students who acknowledge and desire to repent of their honor code violations, rather than continuing to deny what is patently obvious or placing the blame elsewhere, should receive a lesser consequence precisely in order to encourage this habit of the heart. In training students to bring their sin and shame out into the light with respect to these basic classroom matters, we are aiming to instill in them a broader ability to confess and repent of their sins before the Lord and their brothers and sisters in Christ. Of course, this requires a certain level of consistency and approachability from us that will make such a response more likely. Along these lines, as teachers we can model this for our students by apologizing to them when we recognize that we have wronged them in some way. Teachers who open their year by crafting a classroom covenant, as described above, could schedule an occasional check-in to allow themselves and their students to reflect on their commitments and apologize as needed. On a broader level, an institution that is committed to integrity, transparency, and to owning its mistakes publicly when necessary can further cast a vision for this kind of community and build trust with its stakeholders. Through steps such as these, we will be well on our way to making our classrooms and our schools "gardens of delight."

37. See Okholm, *Learning Theology*, 127.
38. Foster, *Celebration of Discipline*, 144.

FORMATIVE PRACTICES OF TIME AND SPACE

Beyond developing and nurturing this kind of approach to community life, teachers can also draw on Benedictine insights to reflect on specific pedagogical practices. In his book *On Christian Teaching*, David Smith challenges Christian teachers to consider how their physical environment impacts learning, emphasizing the formative aspects of how educators make use of time and space.[39] To develop this notion in more detail and to consider various avenues for application, we will in this section consider how Benedict of Nursia, as arguably the most influential Christian educator of all time, ordered time and space in his monasteries in pursuit of forming his monks into Christ's likeness.

Time

From the weekly celebration of Christ's resurrection on Sundays to the early development of the liturgical year, Christianity had already by Benedict's day found ways to order time such that believers could continually enter into key events of salvation history as participants in the divine drama, inhabiting an alternative time governed by Christ himself.[40] While these rhythms have continued to guide the life of the church down through the centuries, it is within the monasteries that we find an approach to time that is most directly applicable for Christian educators. Indeed, a foundational element of Benedict's *Rule* was an intentional approach to the use of time, with Benedict seeking to redeem time itself for the purpose of his monks' spiritual formation (Eph 5:16).

For Benedict, it was crucial that his monastery be a place where "everything may be done at the proper time" (*RB*, §47). By this, Benedict meant that there must be an organized, disciplined pattern of moving through work, study, and prayer each day (and, by extension, each week and each season) that would continually point his monks to the fullness of life in Christ across all aspects of the human person: body, mind, and soul. We are, after all, "essentially rhythmic creatures" who need "rhythm and balance" to grow into the people that we were created to be.[41] Healthy rhythms, then,

---

39. D. Smith, *On Christian Teaching*, 114.

40. On the theological significance of Christian approaches to time, see especially Pfatteicher, *Journey into Heart of God*.

41. See Waal, *Seeking God*, 93; see also Littlejohn and Evans, *Wisdom and Eloquence*, 64–65; Schütz, "To Serve Life," 165–67.

become a means by which we can order time such that time is not wasted and our lives are characterized by order, balance, and spiritual growth.

The rhythm that Benedict is undoubtedly best known for is his precise articulation of eight set services (or "offices") for daily prayer, which he sets out in some detail and which framed the daily life of the monastery (*RB*, §8–18).[42] Because Benedict believed that "nothing is to be preferred to the Work of God" (*RB*, §43), by which in context he meant the divine offices, his monks were called time and again to re-center themselves on the worship of God.[43] The chief formative effects of this way of organizing time are twofold. First, it clearly communicates that the primary purpose of our lives is to worship God. If time itself is a gift from God, it would make sense that giving significant portions of our time back to God in the form of worship would be at the center of our lives, both individually and corporately. Second, the sheer repetition involved in saying these offices day after day contributed to incredible feats of learning. Given that all 150 psalms were recited at least once every week (*RB*, §18), Benedict's monks would have quickly committed the entire psalter to memory, as would have been necessary in an era of high illiteracy and dim lighting. Repetition and memorization get a bad rap in some circles today, but Benedict, like the church fathers more generally, saw these repeated rituals and acts of memorization as a help, and not a hindrance, to learning and to engaging in worship. As Augustine of Hippo argued, the memory is a key means by which we are able to grow and learn, recognize truth, and ascend to God.[44] By deeply imprinting the words, images, and cadences of the psalter into their minds, monks could so internalize this fundamental language of prayer that it would, throughout all the hours of the day, flow from their minds into their hearts and out into their hands.

Beyond the obvious applications with respect to learning more broadly,[45] repetition and memorization can and should be at the heart of training our students in the Scriptures and in prayer.[46] Contrast, for

---

42. Benedict arrived at eight monastic offices in light of the reference to prayer seven times a day in Ps 119:164 plus the reference to prayer in the middle of the night in Ps 119:62 (*RB*, §16).

43. Waal, *Seeking God*, 86. See further Dreher, *Benedict Option*, 57–60.

44. See Augustine, *Confessions*, 10.12–26.

45. See Littlejohn and Evans, *Wisdom and Eloquence*, 165: "Memory is indispensable to learning, and there is no practical definition of learning that does not presuppose that students must remember things."

46. Indeed, memorization is at the heart of how the church has traditionally conceived of catechizing her children; see further Packer and Parrett, *Grounded in the Gospel*, 138–39.

instance, the following two "liturgies" for starting a class period: in Class A, a selected student is called on to offer up a spontaneous prayer for the day ("God, thanks for today, help us on this quiz . . ."); in Class B, the class, together with one voice, recites the Lord's Prayer or the psalm appointed for the day in a lectionary. Which practice would we hope would "stick" with our students long after they have left our classes? Which best points them to truths about Christian community, or about God and his purposes in this world across many different aspects of life? Which will actually *expand* their imagination for prayer, *growing* their vocabulary and fluency in the language of faith? Time spent in repetitive actions need not be an obstacle in the way of deeper learning; rather, it may in fact be an important means by which we bring order and meaning to our days. One of my colleagues, who begins each class by having the entire class stand and recite together the Lord's Prayer, the Apostles' Creed, and Psalm 1, has observed that on those days that he forgets to open with this usual liturgy, students are quick to insist that it take place before class can begin.[47] This liturgy, he believes, allows his students to pause from the pressures of the school day and unite as a community. When reciting these words together, he and his students have to pace themselves and find their shared rhythm for speaking together as a class. It also unites them, in Christ, with the historic body of believers who have recited these same words for centuries, regardless of location or denomination. Such examples help us see that, in structuring the monastery's entire day around prayer, it was clear what—or, better, who—was the center of their life together. If Christ is to be the true center of our classrooms, we too must make conscious decisions to utilize time in such a way that Christ is the priority. This must, of course, go beyond prayer at the start of class; the vision of faith-learning integration that we are developing in this book will help ensure that Christ's presence is felt throughout the entirety of the class period and not just in an opening prayer.

Beyond this essential framework of the daily offices, Benedict also articulates broader daily rhythms that would promote order, balance, and spiritual growth in his monks. Given that "idleness is the enemy of the soul," Benedict insists that his monks "should have specified periods for manual labor as well as for prayerful reading" (*RB*, §48). Work, then, is seen as a natural complement to prayer and study, not as its enemy (hence the later Benedictine motto of *ora et labora*, "prayer and work").[48] This work is therefore not work (or, for that matter, education) as the world knows it, driven

---

47. Sensitive to the likelihood that some of his students may not themselves affirm these words, he requires all of them to stand but explains that their active participation is voluntary.

48. See Chittister, *Wisdom Distilled*, 90; see also Dreher, *Benedict Option*, 60–62.

by a desire for profit and efficiency at the expense of the lives of real human beings; rather, this is work that contributes to human flourishing, both for the individual laborer and for others, in creating things of beauty and value that enrich communities and bless others.[49] To what extent, then, can our teaching engage students in doing real work, work that enriches and blesses other people in real, tangible ways? As we saw in the previous chapter of this book, developing biblical throughlines with a think-feel-act or heads-hearts-hands taxonomy may be one potential way to plan in an intentional manner how to connect our work in the classroom with the real people and needs that exist outside of it. For example, a former colleague who taught creative writing had each of her students visit a local nursing home and listen to one of the residents share his or her life story. The student would then write a poem or short story based on that resident's life experiences, and then return to the nursing home to share the work with the resident whose life inspired the piece of writing. Many of the senior citizens were visibly touched by these students showing interest in their lives (one, amusingly, demanded a rewrite that would be more to his liking!). Not only, though, was this project a very real blessing to the senior citizens who may have otherwise been isolated from young people, but it challenged the students to grow in understanding and empathy for members of the generations that came before them.

Even beyond engaging with time through daily rhythms, Benedict calls us to consider how the changing seasons can shape our practices and develop our spiritual lives. This includes both the cycle of natural seasons, which impacts the quantity and type of labor that we are able to perform (*RB*, §48), and the cycle of the liturgical year, which offers opportunities for special levels of engagement with spiritual disciplines (*RB*, §49).[50] Tish Harrison Warren describes her experience of first engaging with liturgical time as a way of entering into an entirely new way of experiencing time itself:

> Discovering the liturgical calendar felt like discovering real time. It gave a transcendent shape to my life. Time was no longer arbitrary—an academic calendar, a marketing ploy, a back to school sale, a Labor Day blowout, a national holiday, a sports season. Now time was sacred. It was structured by worship. It marked the church as a global, alternative people. Time had shape and meaning. All of a sudden, time was a story. And I could live in a story.[51]

49. See Chittister, *Wisdom Distilled*, 91–94; see also Waal, *Seeking God*, 108–11.

50. On the liturgical year, see further, e.g., Black, *Welcome to the Church Year*; Pfatteicher, *Journey into Heart of God*.

51. Warren, *Liturgy of the Ordinary*, 106.

Indeed, as discussed in the previous chapter of this book, at the heart of Christian theology lies a story: the story of creation, fall, redemption, and consummation. By embracing this story as their own, students are called to repent of their sins, acknowledge Jesus as King, and reorder their lives in accordance with their identity as citizens of the kingdom of God, living as the people of God for the sake of others. What Warren is pointing us to, then, is an understanding that the church's liturgical year can, like the biblical throughlines described above, provide entry points into this story. How, then, might the rhythms of our classroom feel different, say, in Advent or Lent versus in Epiphany or Eastertide? Do our students even know there is a different way to move through time that makes the great feasts and fasts of the church year, and not long weekends or semester-end exams, the most significant dates that we anticipate? To return to the example of a liturgy for beginning class, even something as small as having these prayers change with the seasons of the church year could help communicate the existence and significance of this distinctively Christian way of ordering time. Additionally, the liturgical year could even drive the types of assignments we design; in Epiphany, for instance, we might encourage students to engage with non-Christians in the wider community as a way of engaging with the evangelistic theme of that season.

In sum, Benedict challenges us to consider how our decisions about the use of time can contribute to the spiritual formation of our learners. In closing this section, I want to consider one specific way in which the Benedictine approach to time, namely its emphasis on order and balance when it comes to work and rest, might inform our pedagogy. As I have argued elsewhere, "The most urgent and most significant task of this generation is to recover, amidst a culture that prizes speed and efficiency, and amidst a world that ceaselessly clamors for our constant attention through new digital technologies, a way of life that allows us to set aside the distractions of this world in order to ascend to God."[52] To what extent, we might ask, does our classroom culture as it relates to how we use time work towards or against this way of life? One way we can measure this is to consider the amount of space we make in our classroom for stillness and silence. Engaging in times of stillness and quiet was, for Benedict, a non-negotiable element of monastic spirituality (*RB*, §6), though for many it can be scary to be left alone with one's own thoughts.[53] I think this is precisely the reason so many of my students fall asleep listening to Spotify playlists or streaming Netflix on their phones—anything to drown out the voices within. Students,

52. Hughes, *How Spirit Became God*, 138.
53. See Chittister, *Wisdom Distilled*, 169.

then, need silence even if (and maybe especially if) they do not want it, and the classroom can be a place where they can learn to sit with themselves and their thoughts in a way that prepares them for a life of prayer and contemplation.

On the smallest level, for instance, we may wish to allow more time for students to respond to a question, giving a larger set of students an opportunity to organize their thoughts and participate in the classroom discussion simply by allowing (or requiring) there to be an extended period of pause before permitting students to raise their hands.[54] Here a spiritual truth directly correlates with what most educators would agree to be good pedagogy; not giving our students adequate time to formulate meaningful responses will, as David Smith explains, "reinforce habits of reading quickly, skimming for answers, and speaking out before thinking carefully, habits that seem at odds with the kind of attentiveness that might characterize an approach grounded in charity and justice."[55] We might also consider how we can incorporate silence as part of the rhythms of a class period as a whole. I have found the practice of having students keep reflection journals to be one simple yet effective way of building structures that train students in the disciplines of quiet and stillness. If we are honest with ourselves, I expect we will find that rushing to fit in a final ten minutes of a lecture is less helpful for student learning than allowing students to take those final minutes to review and synthesize what they have learned in the day's lesson. Finally, we can think of novel ways to incorporate more extended periods of stillness and quiet over the course of an entire semester or academic year. Smith provocatively suggests that whereas church liturgies conclude with "a blessing and a commission," school semesters end with "a judgment and a dismissal."[56] Finding creative ways to incorporate quiet reflection (especially as it is then paired with communal celebration!) at the conclusion of an academic term may, therefore, further contribute to developing a classroom culture that enables students to engage with habits of stillness and silence that will hopefully extend into their broader lives. To this end, schools that conclude their spring semester with a retreat for graduating seniors, and incorporate within that retreat opportunities for quiet reflection on their educational and spiritual journeys over the course of their lives, are providing opportunities for such a concluding blessing and commission.

54. See D. Smith, *On Christian Teaching*, 120–21.

55. D. Smith, *On Christian Teaching*, 121.

56. D. Smith, *On Christian Teaching*, 124. On rhythms of work and rest in the classroom, see further D. Smith and Felch, *Teaching and Christian Imagination*, 84–86.

Space

Along with its intentional engagement with time, the Christian tradition has consistently affirmed the importance of critical reflection on the use of space. In fact, the church has historically connected liturgical space with liturgical time; as James K. A. Smith writes, physical changes in the sanctuary over the course of the church year demonstrate that "just the space of worship would tell a story that actually organizes time—an indication that here dwells a people with a unique sense of *temporality*, who inhabit a time that is out of joint with the regular, mundane ticking of commercial time or the standard shape of the academic year."[57] Moving outside the walls of the church into the everyday world, we find that just as Benedict's *Rule* seeks to redeem all of time for the purposes of spiritual formation, so also it envisions ways in which the use of physical space can point to Christ.

Benedict posits that even matters as seemingly mundane as the monks' sleeping arrangements can be a means of mutual encouragement and edification; by interspersing the younger monks' beds among those of the older ones, for instance, the older monks would be better able to rouse their younger brothers at the appointed times for prayer, "for the sleepy like to make excuses" (*RB*, §22). Likewise, Benedict insists on having a separate kitchen set aside for the exclusive use of the abbot and the guests of the monastery, so that the arrival of guests at unusual times will not "disturb the brothers" (*RB*, §53). By physically separating the kitchens for normal use and for guests, Benedict aims to safeguard the rhythms of the divine office while providing hospitality in something of a liminal space for guests who are honored and yet not bound to follow the *Rule* itself. On a broader level, the arrangement of the monastery in its entirety must be done with careful forethought. As Benedict instructs, "The monastery should, if possible, be so constructed that within it all necessities, such as water, mill and garden are contained, and the various crafts are practiced. Then there will be no need for the monks to roam outside, because this is not at all good for their souls" (*RB*, §66). Lest the monks be exposed to negative influences or temptations outside the protective walls of the monastery, the design of the monastery was such that there was no need for monks to leave it.

Thus, the *Rule* helps us see that the way in which we set up and arrange the physical spaces of our classrooms sends formative messages to our students. As observed above with reference to Chrysostom's gate of the eyes, the objects we hang or display in our classrooms have the potential to cultivate

57. J. Smith, *Desiring the Kingdom*, 156 (italics in original).

our students' appetites for what is true, good, and beautiful.[58] Likewise, Benedict's intentional arrangement of beds to intersperse the young and the old can challenge us to think about how to purposefully arrange seating to maximize collaboration within groups of students at different levels of aptitude. Furthermore, Benedict's insistence on hospitality for pilgrims enables us to consider how the arrangement of the physical space of our classrooms can contribute to establishing what David Smith calls "hospitable spaces for students on their educational journeys."[59] Referring to the *Rule*, Smith casts the teacher as a Benedictine guestmaster, providing safety, refreshment, and nourishment for his pilgrim-students.[60] From this perspective, then, even simple actions such as setting out a pot of coffee for an early morning class of sleepy, stressed seniors, placing couches and overstuffed chairs in the back of the room on which students may rest and socialize between classes, and arranging desks so that students are facing one another and not simply the teacher—all communicate that this classroom is a physical space where students, as embodied beings, are welcomed, where everything is prepared for them, and where they can find respite and connection with one another. Finally, Benedict's instructions to have all necessary provisions on hand so monks will not need to leave the monastery can illuminate some of our current debates about technology use in the classroom: is technology, for instance, keeping students focused on what is taking place in the physical space around them, or is it transporting their minds to "outside" the walls of the classroom where they can "roam" into alleyways where they should not go? As educators, we increasingly "need to figure out how to connect and balance engagement with the world, protection from the world, moral boundaries, and acceptance of failure and limitations."[61] Benedict's image certainly suggests a more guarded posture towards such outside influences, and yet he is not preparing his monks to go back out into the world in the same way that Christian schools aspire to prepare students for navigating the challenges of the world after graduation. Still, this provocative image should challenge us to give careful consideration to how we can wisely discern the appropriate use of technology as one element of how we approach the issue of "space" in a digital age.[62]

---

58. See again Chrysostom, "Vain.," §55–62; cf. Littlejohn and Evans, *Wisdom and Eloquence*, 67.

59. D. Smith and Felch, *Teaching and Christian Imagination*, 67.

60. See D. Smith and Felch, *Teaching and Christian Imagination*, 69–71. On Benedictine hospitality, see also Chittister, *Wisdom Distilled*, 121–32.

61. D. Smith et al., *Digital Life Together*, 173.

62. See further D. Smith et al., *Digital Life Together*, 137–97.

Returning to the *Rule* itself, Benedict suggests that it is not merely the arrangement of physical things that matter but also the way in which those physical things that fill our space are treated. Because everything in the monastery belongs to God, Benedict can demand that the monastery's cellarer must "regard all utensils and goods of the monastery as sacred vessels of the altar" (*RB*, §31). Similarly, all monks are responsible for the tools and clothing that have been lent to them: "Whoever fails to keep the things belonging to the monastery clean or treats them carelessly should be reproved" (*RB*, §32).[63] Benedict's ultimate concern with such instructions is that, in the model of the primitive church (Acts 4:32), "no one may presume to give, receive or retain anything as his own, nothing at all—not a book, writing tablets, or stylus—in short, not a single item" (*RB*, §33). While other monastic orders took vows of radical poverty, the Benedictine approach to possessions is more nuanced. What matters is not so much whether one has possessions or not but whether one has the ability to enjoy them with a proper sense of detachment.[64] Enjoyment of God's good gifts is, after all, itself an act of worship. Against a world-denying attitude, Benedict is essentially calling his monks to a sacramental view of the material world, such that even the most ordinary physical goods are "symbols that reveal the beauty and the goodness of their creator."[65] It is, therefore, not simply how physical space is arranged that matters to Benedict but also what physical objects are in that space and the manner in which they are used.

We encourage our students to take such an approach to possessions when, like Benedict's monks, they are challenged to take ownership and responsibility for the space in which they learn and the physical objects that fill that space. Encouraging students to take responsibility for their actions and for stewarding the community's resources, even in the simplest ways, such as mandating that students clean up after themselves, pushes back on their innate tendencies towards entitlement and self-centeredness. By requiring all students to participate in chores around the school, such as cleaning hallways or raking leaves during fall, we have the opportunity to train our students to find value, and perhaps even some amount of enjoyment, in hard work that builds up the community as a whole.

The above applications from the *Rule* of St. Benedict presume an actual physical classroom environment. The COVID-19 pandemic has, of course, challenged educators' abilities to foster hospitable classroom spaces

63. Thus, anyone who breaks or loses something must immediately tell the abbot and assign himself a penance (*RB*, §46).

64. See Waal, *Seeking God*, 101–2.

65. Waal, *Seeking God*, 104; cf. Chittister, *Wisdom Distilled*, 95–96.

amidst social distancing guidelines, if students were even able to gather in-person in the first place. But even before the advent of this long, arduous season of COVIDtide, many Christian teachers, particularly at the university level, have been assigned an increasing number of hybrid or fully online classes. What, then, would it look like to reflect on how virtual "space" can be put to spiritually formative purposes? While a full discussion of this issue is beyond the scope of this book, Kristen Ferguson has set out a basic framework for "building online courses with strategic interaction, resulting in community with missional impact," suggesting that careful attention to course design, delivery, and program management can work towards many of the same goals we would have for in-person learners.[66] At minimum, we can give careful consideration to intentionally and strategically designing learning experiences that foster meaningful connections between the teacher and student or among students.[67] We can, moreover, apply the same level of strategic planning to thinking about how our assignments could connect students with real people and real needs in the world, recognizing that "online students do not need to be in front of their computers for the entire online course," and thereby extending the "space" in which the class takes place out of the purely virtual realm into the embodied existence of reality.[68] While details of how to implement such a framework will no doubt depend in large part on different institutional contexts and technological systems, we can be confident that even our online spaces have the potential to be characterized by spiritually formative approaches to community life and the use of space and time. Even in such a context, then, we can push our learners to spiritual disciplines; for instance, exhorting students to take a "sabbath rest from technology," reinforced by thoughtful attention to due dates and by choosing when new materials are made available, can challenge them to engage with this formative practice of the Christian life.[69] Careful reflection and intentionality, then, would appear to be key in thinking about the "space" of online learning, just as they have value in a traditional classroom environment.

66. Ferguson, *Excellence in Online Education*, 43.

67. See Ferguson, *Excellence in Online Education*, 72–75. See also D. Smith et al., *Digital Life Together*, 272–79.

68. Ferguson, *Excellence in Online Education*, 75. See also D. Smith et al., *Digital Life Together*, 208–22.

69. D. Smith et al., *Digital Life Together*, 240.

PEDAGOGY, REIMAGINED

In this chapter, we have aimed at reimagining how our classrooms can become harmonious communities in which each of our students is assisted in his or her spiritual formation. As in Benedict's monastery, all of our pedagogical choices implicitly communicate a greater *telos*, meaning that the way in which we go about the process of teaching and learning has the potential to be just as formational for our students as the curriculum we teach or the relationships we form with our students. Through our examination of major elements of the *Rule* of St. Benedict, we have identified key aspects of our pedagogy, such as our use of time and space, shared practices, and approach to discipline, that have the potential to shape our students into Christ's likeness. When this approach to pedagogy aligns with the design of curriculum described in the previous chapter of this book, we unleash a powerful synergy by which the Holy Spirit may move our students forward on the path of discipleship. Throughout this book, we have alluded to growth in the way of discipleship as the primary goal that we as Christian educators have for our students and have begun to put forward some specific elements by which we might advance that particular aim, and yet we have not to this point directly addressed the specific outcomes and processes that might provide an overarching framework for this approach. In the next chapter of this book, then, we will need to pull together all of the threads that we have begun to set out in order to develop a specific, actionable vision for what we are trying to accomplish with our students in regards to spiritual formation at the institutional level.

6

How Do We Plan for Growth?

Cyril of Jerusalem and Catechesis by Design

We have now not only reimagined the identities of teachers and students but also considered how careful attention to matters of curriculum and pedagogy can contribute to our students' spiritual formation. The focus, thus far, has been on the individual teacher and his or her classroom as a place where spiritual formation takes place. At this point, however, we will shift gears to consider how, at an institutional level, a broader strategic approach to spiritual formation can not only help guide the decisions of individual teachers but also ensure an overall design that works towards a clear and consistent vision of spiritual growth. Apart from an explicitly stated understanding of what we mean by spiritual growth, we risk a diminishment of the *telos* of our education to some variant of moralistic therapeutic deism or to the simple hope that our students will feel warm and fuzzy feelings about Jesus. Moreover, a lack of willingness to reflect critically on whether or not our efforts at spiritual formation are amounting to anything undoubtedly inhibits our ability to adapt and refine the structures that would guide any such approach. As a result, what we need is a clear and reinvigorated vision for the spiritual outcomes to which Christian education is to aspire, as well as a set of benchmarks by which we can measure if our efforts are bearing any fruit. Drawing on the various elements discussed thus far in this book, we can begin designing an actionable plan by which an institution can, through the power of the Holy Spirit, move its students along in their spiritual journeys and cultivate a posture of continuous reflection on the role of its faculty, staff, and administrators in that process. These concerns, not developed in great detail in many contemporary works on the integration of faith and learning, were nevertheless very important to the early church fathers.[1] As we will discover in this chapter, the ancient catechumenate, as illuminated by Cyril of Jerusalem's "Procatechesis," provides us with a model and a foundation for articulating and evaluating our own institutions' efforts at contributing to our students' spiritual formation.

From the Greek word meaning "to teach," catechesis in early Christianity referred to not merely instruction in the essential truth claims of the Christian faith but also training in an entirely different way of life. Specifically, this would come to refer to a fixed period of instruction (typically somewhere between one to three years) in preparation for baptism that emerged around the middle of the second century.[2] The development of the catechumenate, as it was known, was almost certainly in response to increasing interest in Christianity from pagans with little to no familiarity with the church's teachings and practices. In light of this, what was needed was what Gerald Sittser describes as "a rigorous training program to form people in the faith, to prepare them for church membership, and to equip them to be effective witnesses in the empire."[3] The brilliance of the catechumenate was that it established an inviting space for experiencing the Christian life, creating "permeable boundaries" that could bridge the pagan world with the world of the church, allowing interested outsiders to immerse themselves in the Christian way of life without having made the final commitment of baptism.[4] The catechumenate, therefore, may have functioned roughly akin to a modern language immersion program in which students acquire increasing degrees of fluency as they are plunged headfirst into a foreign culture.[5] In

---

1. Such discussions tend to draw much more on the insights of modern science than on the historic teachings of the church; see, e.g., the summary of various modern proposals in Pazmiño, *Foundational Issues*, 213–19. For one new approach to this issue, see the Practicing Faith Survey created by the Kuyers Institute at Calvin University and Cardus Education and managed by the Center for the Advancement of Christian Education at Dordt University (explore online at https://practicing.faith).

2. For a historical overview of the development of the catechumenate, with attention to contemporary applications, see Arnold, "Early Church Catechesis," 42–53; Sittser, *Resilient Faith*, 155–72; Packer and Parrett, *Grounded in the Gospel*, 51–73. The classic ancient account of the early catechumenate is found in the *Apostolic Tradition*, §15–21, a text traditionally attributed to Hippolytus of Rome and dated to the third century.

3. Sittser, *Resilient Faith*, 157.

4. Sittser, *Resilient Faith*, 157.

5. See Sittser, *Resilient Faith*, 157–58. This idea of learning Christianity as akin to acquiring foreign language proficiency is developed in, e.g., Vanderstelt, *Gospel Fluency*, 37–45.

sum, catechesis was an intentional strategy for making disciples in the early church, characterized not just by the transmission of knowledge but also by engagement with the work of spiritual formation.

Among the many important catechetical writings of the early church, the catechetical lectures of Cyril of Jerusalem (ca. 313–86), delivered sometime around the middle of the fourth century, have long been considered classics of their genre.[6] Likely a native of Jerusalem, Cyril became bishop in the wake of the Emperor Constantine's grand church-building program in the holy city and in the midst of the intrigues of the Arian controversy.[7] Of particular interest is his "Procatechesis," which Cyril delivered at the beginning of the Lenten season to a group of catechumens who had enrolled to become candidates for baptism, which would take place on the coming Easter.[8] This address set the foundation for all of Cyril's subsequent catechetical teaching, providing an overview of the forthcoming instruction that Cyril would give in the weeks and days leading up to their baptism.[9] Like many of those to whom Cyril spoke, our students today, whether they would identify as Christian or not, increasingly have little knowledge of the doctrines and practices of biblical, historic Christianity. This lack of preliminary engagement with the Christian faith reflects broader challenges in our culture today, and yet when viewed through the right lens it can in fact be recognized as a powerful opportunity for Christian educators. In particular, we will find that Cyril's understanding of catechesis as a means of progressing through faith development stages can help us understand the nature and goal of spiritual formation and develop strategies to engage our students' heads, hearts, and hands with the Holy Spirit.

6. For a defense of Cyrilline authorship of this and the other catechetical lectures traditionally ascribed to Cyril, see Johnson, "Introduction," 35–55; Yarnold, *Cyril of Jerusalem*, 22–32. A more detailed and scholarly introduction to Cyril's catechetical lectures, with special attention to their historical context, can be found in Kalleres, "Cultivating True Sight."

7. For an introduction to Cyril's life and the city of Jerusalem in the fourth century, see Johnson, "Introduction," 18–21; Yarnold, *Cyril of Jerusalem*, 3–21.

8. Technically, at this point they would no longer be catechumens but *phōtizomenoi* ("ones being enlightened"; "Procat.," §1), corresponding to the Latin equivalent of *competentes* ("seekers"). For simplicity's sake, I will continue to call them catechumens over the course of this chapter.

9. On the liturgy surrounding the catechumenate and baptism in Cyril's Jerusalem, see Johnson, "Introduction," 21–34; Yarnold, *Cyril of Jerusalem*, 33–55.

SPIRITUAL FORMATION AS A
JOURNEY FROM DEATH TO LIFE

On first glance, Cyril's "Procatechesis" does not appear to have a clear connection with the work of a Christian school. In terms of subject matter, the
first section of this address ("Procat.," §1–8) is an exhortation to catechumens to reflect on their motives for pursuing baptism and to seize the opportunity afforded by this period of preparation to purify their hearts and
pursue Christ with single-mindedness. While Cyril is writing in a specific
liturgical context in a particular time and place, we will find that the vision
of the spiritual life that he sets forth can nevertheless challenge Christian
schools to have a better understanding of the nature of spiritual formation,
making it evident that *all* of our students are "catechumens" on a lifelong
journey of faith who will benefit from engagement with Christian teachings
and practices.

The Time of Decision

Cyril opens his "Procatechesis" with a summary of his audience's present
spiritual state. Speaking at the outset of his address to this group of catechumens who have written down their names as candidates for baptism, he
notes that, while there is much for which to commend them at the present
time, they yet lack a fullness that is needed for their further progression in
the faith: "Already the sweet smell of blessedness is upon you, O you who
are being enlightened; already you are gathering invisible flowers for the
weaving of heavenly crowns. Already the fragrant aroma of the Holy Spirit
has breathed upon you. Already you have come to the entrance hall of the
king's palace. Let it be also that the king leads you inside. For now the buds
of the trees are visible; let it be for the perfection of the fruit" ("Procat.,"
§1).[10] One pivotal insight we can glean from these opening words concerns
the notion of stages of faith development. Among many Christian educators, there is an unfortunate tendency to try to group students into one of
two groups: "saved" and "unsaved," or, to use different terms, "believers" and
"non-believers," based solely on our judgment of their spiritual conditions.
Cyril, however, has a more complex understanding of the process of faith
formation, allowing for the existence of a liminal stage in which people are
attracted to and show interest in the Christian faith without having made a
decisive commitment to Christ through baptism.

---

10. All quotations of the "Procatechesis" are taken from the translation of Johnson.

Is it fair, then, to speak of Cyril's catechumens as genuine Christians? The answer to this question hinges in large part on one's understanding of the relationship between baptism and regeneration, a topic which is beyond the scope of this chapter.[11] Regardless, even those who may not fully adopt Cyril's understanding of baptism will likely affirm that part of the brilliance of the ancient Christian catechumenate was its creation of a liminal stage between "outsiders" and "insiders" of the faith. As such, Cyril can speak of the catechumens as in the process of "being enlightened" without having reached the fulfillment of such a process. Thus, he argues, they are like visitors to a royal palace who are in the entrance hall but have not yet been invited in by the king; they are like trees on which buds have appeared but the fruit has not yet appeared. There is, on the one hand, an acknowledgment that God is already active in beginning to draw these individuals to himself, while on the other there is a clear recognition that they do not yet fully belong to him. They are, in fact, poised between two worlds, as God "looks for the genuine decision of each one" ("Procat.," §1), to see which path they will take at this key junction in their lives.

Cyril's tone throughout this section, and indeed the entire address, is one of "great warmth," helping us to understand that even those later sections that may appear harsh should be interpreted through this tone which was in fact characteristic of most early Christian catechetical lectures.[12] Cyril's insights can help us strike a similar tone with all of the students attending our institutions as we reflect on the variety of places where they find themselves on their spiritual journeys. Like a coach who has athletes of vastly different abilities and levels of interest on his team, and yet nevertheless aims to move all of them forward into better knowledge of the sport and greater skill in playing the game, we can see all of our learners as in need of further spiritual formation. Rather than lament the spiritual condition of the "lost souls" brought into the midst of our school community, we can instead be grateful for the opportunity to be able to play a role in the great adventure of their spiritual development.

The church has long recognized that there are various stages of spiritual development that characterize the journey to Christian maturity. Through the centuries, Christian writers have proposed various models that aim to provide, in general terms, the essential signposts along the path of spiritual growth.[13] Appropriating this idea of the stages of faith formation is a helpful

---

11. See Arnold, "Early Church Catechesis," 42–43.

12. Harmless, *Augustine and the Catechumenate*, 77.

13. See, e.g., the overview of historical models in Demarest, *Seasons of the Soul*, 160–69.

and particularly appropriate way to make sense of the likely spiritual status of much of our student population, for in many respects, Cyril's description of his catechumens largely rings true to my own sense of the high school students that I teach. By their very nature as teenagers, my students exist in a liminal space between childhood and adulthood, having been exposed to the faith of their parents, teachers, and pastors, but now standing on the precipice of deciding if they are going to be led inside the king's palace, take up their crosses, and bear the fruit of the Spirit.[14] The time for decision, for many of our students as for Cyril's catechumens, is very much at hand. To use the athletic image above, the season is starting now, and the athletes need to decide if they want to take the field for an actual competitive match that will involve some amount of risk and sacrifice. Outside of the class-room, some may be deciding to pursue adult baptism, be confirmed in their church, or simply cement if faith will even be a priority as they come into their own as young adults. It is certainly the case that God tells very long stories and we do not know exactly the course that any one person's spiritual journey will take, and yet the decisions that young adults make will very much set up their lives for certain trajectories, and thus a decision for Christ in this stage of life can do much to start sending down roots that will lead to much fruit and righteousness (Ps 1:1–4).

The need for such a genuine decision is underscored by Cyril's concern that some in his audience might not be fully present at his catechetical lectures or might not be present for the right reasons. As Cyril tells his catechumens, "For although your body might be here, if your mind is not, nothing is gained" ("Procat.," §1). Thus, he appeals to the example of Simon Magus, who was "baptized but not enlightened" to demonstrate that the sacrament of baptism, apart from a right intention, avails nothing ("Procat.," §2; cf. Acts 8:9–24). Likewise, Cyril points to the man in Jesus's parable of the wedding feast who came without a wedding garment and was cast out into the outer darkness as a further example of the need to proceed with right intentions ("Procat.," §3; cf. Matt 22:1–14). Cyril is particularly concerned that some might be seeking baptism without the intention of repenting of their sins; the season of Lent, then, becomes the perfect opportunity to put aside those things that constitute an "evil intention" ("Procat.," §4). Besides this, Cyril is concerned that some of his catechumens might be pursuing baptism for the wrong reasons. Perhaps, he suggests, some of the men are seeking baptism solely to please or impress a woman, or vice versa. Cyril is

14. This is true of younger students, too, to the extent that the "habits of the heart" that they are forming at an early age will very much influence their future course in life.

happy in this case to "accept the bait from the fishhook" and engage them as catechumens despite their "false motive" ("Procat.," §5).[15]

Again, setting aside the liturgical context of Cyril's address, we see many parallels between his catechumens and our students. After all, how many of our students' bodies are physically present in schools, and yet their minds are not? What Cyril told his catechumens is just as true for our students: if they have been baptized, confirmed, go to church, or graduate from a Christian school but lack an inner heart transformation, it gains them nothing. How many of our students are only in our buildings because this is the education that their parents have selected for them? How many of them feign interest in spiritual matters to impress us or to get good grades? How many of them lack a keen understanding of their own sinfulness or the desire to grow in repentance and righteousness? Cyril's introduction makes clear that *all* his catechumens have failed to achieve the single-mindedness that is at the heart of the Christian life. None of them can claim to have arrived on the journey of faith—some, it appears, have hardly endeavored to begin— and yet Cyril engages them all with the call to discipleship. Cyril's words to his catechumens thus suggest that if we too view discipleship as having early stages by which our students gain initial exposure to the Christian way, we need not wonder if our efforts at spiritual formation should be reserved for one particular group of students. Rather, we can rest on the assumption that all of the students under our care (like all of us!) need continual training in how to be a Christian and need to be immersed in Scripture, theology, and the practices of spiritual formation, praying that the Holy Spirit will work through these things to draw them ever nearer to the Lord.[16]

The Purgation of Sin

Having ascertained his catechumens' present undeveloped state of spiritual formation, Cyril proceeds to articulate the desired outcome he intends to find in those who will be admitted to baptism. Cyril's beautiful imagery is worth quoting at length ("Procat.," §5): "You have come into the nets of the

---

15. As Yarnold suggests, the fact that such catechumens were enrolled for baptism in the first place contrasts with the more rigorous process of admission described by Egeria later in the fourth century, suggesting an evolution in Cyril's own practice over the decades (Yarnold, *Cyril of Jerusalem*, 35–36).

16. See Arnold, "Early Church Catechesis," 46–51. To draw on more technical language, I thus see catechesis as having a dual purpose as outlined in Packer and Scandrett, eds., *To Be a Christian*, 137: catechesis encompasses both "catechetical evangelism" (or catechesis "from the front porch") and "liturgical catechesis" (or catechesis "from the font"). See also Littlejohn and Evans, *Wisdom and Eloquence*, 46.

Church. Be caught! Stop fleeing! For is not Jesus catching you, not that you might die, but that in dying you might be made alive? For it is necessary for you to die and to rise. For you have heard the Apostle saying, 'dead to sin but living to righteousness' [Rom 6:11]. Die, then, to sins, and live to righteousness! From today on, live!" The Christian life is thus understood by Cyril primarily through the lens of dying to self and living in Christ, as evidenced in a turning away from sin and a pursuit of righteousness, and as enacted sacramentally at baptism. Paul makes this connection explicit earlier in this same chapter of his letter to the Romans when he writes, "Do you not know that all of us who have been baptized into Christ Jesus were baptized into his death? We were buried therefore with him by baptism into death, in order that, just as Christ was raised from the dead by the glory of the Father, we too might walk in newness of life" (Rom 6:3–4). While this is not the only baptismal image in early Christianity, Robin Jensen nevertheless concludes that "the theme of baptismal death and rebirth appears in the earliest strands of Christian teaching and is, arguably, the most transformative dimension of early Christian initiation."[17]

While baptism was thus understood to be the sacramental means of this death-to-life transformation, Cyril nevertheless calls his catechumens to the mortification of sin even prior to their baptism.[18] Thus, just as a couple engaged to be married is to have single-minded devotion to preparing for their wedding feast, so also Cyril calls his catechumens to the pursuit of "spiritual things" in light of the sacrament that would soon unite them to Christ, the "heavenly Bridegroom" ("Procat.," §6); after all, baptism is a singular, unrepeatable event in the life of a believer ("Procat.," §7). In light of the great seriousness of the sacrament, Cyril continues, the catechumens must put away whatever evil intentions they brought with them and instead die to sin, beginning that very day. As Cyril simply puts it, "From today on abstain from every evil thing. Let your tongue not speak insignificant words, nor let your sight look at sin, nor let your mind wander toward what is not profitable" ("Procat.," §8). By so repenting, the catechumens would demonstrate the good intention that they presently lack and be rightly prepared for baptism.[19]

17. Jensen, *Baptismal Imagery*, 137. For how this theme impacted early Christian art, architecture, and ritual actions associated with baptism, see Jensen, *Baptismal Imagery*, 149–75.

18. See McGowan, *Ancient Christian Worship*, 168: "Baptism stood at the completion of a process wherein lifestyles, as well as beliefs, were examined and changed; yet it was not merely a symbolic confirmation of those changes but an objective encounter with divine grace, forgiveness, and renewal."

19. For Cyril's own baptismal liturgy, see Yarnold, *Cyril of Jerusalem*, 39–40.

Cyril's emphasis on the purgation of sin as the initial stage of spiritual growth is very much characteristic of most patristic and medieval approaches to spiritual development. In this classical "Triple Way" paradigm of purgation, illumination, and contemplation, this first phase involves "conversion to Christ, purification of sins and self-denial by the practice of spiritual disciplines, including prayer and loosening attachment to material things."[20] The ascetical practices of the early church fathers, which have been referenced throughout this book, are thus very much a central part of the church's traditional path to spiritual maturity insofar as they provide a means of increasingly rooting out those sinful thoughts, words, and deeds that keep us from the fullness of life in Christ. Crucially, the mortification of sin is not an end in its own right; rather, it is one of the key means by which we cooperate with the Holy Spirit in working towards our God-given *telos*, which Cyril describes as union with Christ.[21] Thus, Cyril and the other church fathers remind us that the struggle against sin and our growth in holiness is actually the beginning, and not the end, of the Christian life. On a broader level, Cyril is reminding us that the Christian life into which we wish to catechize our students and ourselves is not simply one of acquiring information about God or even of having happy feelings about God; rather, it is a distinctive way of being (fully!) human that has implications for every aspect of our lives. Thus, while the purgative aspect of catechesis is perhaps the most neglected under the present reign of moralistic therapeutic deism, for the early Christians, this was a central part of the catechumenate; a catechumen's lifestyle, vocation, and behaviors were all subject to intense scrutiny by church leaders.[22] The purgation of sin was therefore the foundational element demanded of those who desired to walk the Christian way, and the retrieval of this idea can stimulate our thinking about our desired student learning outcomes.

I suspect that part of our reluctance to engage our students in the work of purgation stems from our greatly diminished understanding of sin. Our society—and by extension, many of our churches and schools—treats many human failings not as spiritual matters which require repentance and forgiveness but as challenges that can be overcome through the latest self-help book or social media fad (that is, if they are even seen as failings in the first place). This is, of course, a key feature of our therapeutic culture; as Christian Smith and Melinda Lundquist Denton write, "many activities and

20. Demarest, *Seasons of the Soul*, 161. We need not completely adapt this paradigm to recognize the centrality of purgation for the spirituality of the early church.
21. See again "Procat.," §6.
22. See Arnold, "Early Church Catechesis," 49.

behaviors once defined as moral failures . . . are redefined as either perfectly legitimate 'lifestyles' or as psychological and medical dysfunctions, diseases, syndromes, codependencies, or pathologies."[23] Moreover, in a postmodern world that rejects "right" and "wrong" in favor of moral relativism, identifying and calling out "sin" appears to many to be insensitive, intolerant, and detrimental to a person's self-esteem. For the early church fathers, however, the battle against sin was at the center of the Christian spiritual journey; in their understanding, explains Andrew McGowan, sin was "not mere events or specific actions but whole ways of thinking and acting."[24] The fathers have left us many writings that both synthesize and systematize the Bible's teaching on sin. It is, in fact, precisely this focus on sin that allows the church fathers to develop a corresponding emphasis on virtue as the means of growing into the Christian way of life.

To take just one significant example from the patristic period, *The Conferences* of John Cassian (ca. 360–435), dating from the early fifth century, includes a substantial discussion of what Cassian, in a section he attributes to the desert father Abba Serapion, identifies as the "eight principal vices that attack humankind."[25] These are, on the one hand, carnal vices such as gluttony and fornication, while other vices, such as pride and vainglory, are spiritual in nature. Likewise, Cassian distinguishes between those vices that have external causes, such as avarice and anger, and those that have internal causes, such as acedia (that is, sloth or apathy) and sorrow.[26] In articulating the causes and suggested remedies for each of these vices, Cassian anticipates Gregory the Great's approach to spiritual direction, as described in an earlier chapter of this book.[27] Likewise, Cassian's attention to vices such as vainglory, avarice, and pride parallels similar treatments of those themes that we have already explored in, respectively, the writings of Chrysostom, Basil, and Benedict. This observation indicates that Cassian's collection of vices was not haphazard or arbitrary but rather reflects a fairly stable and consistent understanding of vice that has endured throughout the Christian

23. C. Smith and Denton, *Soul Searching*, 173. This is not, of course, to deny that many people suffer from real medical conditions; the point is simply that, in some circumstances, lack of personal moral responsibility as a contributing factor to certain issues is overlooked.

24. McGowan, *Ancient Christian Worship*, 151.

25. Cassian, *Conferences*, 5.2. All quotations of *The Conferences* are taken from the translation of Ramsey. In terms of form, this text purports to be a recollection of a series of dialogues between Cassian and various monks who lived in the Egyptian desert.

26. Cassian, *Conferences*, 5.3.

27. Gregory himself was deeply impacted by Cassian and reformulated Cassian's list into its familiar form today of the "seven deadly sins," in which pride is identified as the root of all the other sins.

tradition via works such as Thomas Aquinas's *Summa Theologica*, Dante's *Divine Comedy*, and Chaucer's *Canterbury Tales*.[28] Thus, when we read Cyril charging his catechumens to die to sin, we can put some meat on the otherwise abstract bones of sin by thinking about the need to die to these specific traditional vices.

Cassian also makes explicit what Cyril leaves largely implicit with respect to the purgation of sin being a means towards a greater end rather than an end in and of itself. As Cassian writes, retelling the words of Abba Moses, "The end of our profession, as we have said, is the kingdom of God or the kingdom of heaven; but the goal or scopos is purity of heart, without which it is impossible for anyone to reach that end."[29] That is to say, the Christian life and the purgation of sin required of all believers is a means of reaching our immediate "goal" (*skopos*) of purity of heart, which in turn works towards the ultimate "end" (*telos*) of our union with God in his eternal kingdom. It may be tempting to push ourselves and our students directly to kingdom work, but Cassian correctly saw that we are actually more likely to reach our God-given *telos* when we focus on the intermediary work of purgation. In such an approach, when we allow kingdom work to flow from a clear vision of the kingdom itself, we have the best chances of avoiding either a brittle fundamentalism and legalism on the one hand or a reductive social justice movement on the other.[30]

Indeed, it is precisely as we engage with this difficult work of pruning away that which keeps us from purity of heart and single-minded devotion to God that we will discover the path to progress in virtue and spiritual maturity. This connection between purgation, virtue, and union with Christ is well-illustrated by Cyril's use of the imagery of changing one's garments; for instance, Cyril tells them, "If avarice is the garment of your soul, put on another and come in" to the wedding feast where Jesus, the bridegroom, awaits ("Procat.," §4; cf. Matt 22:1–14). Virtue, it would appear, cannot be achieved without an explicit turning away from sin, a point which Paul himself develops at some length (Gal 5:16–26).

At this point, we must briefly pause to address a potential concern that some evangelical readers might have: does not this language of striving to purge ourselves of sin detract from the Protestant understanding of justification by faith alone? By no means: while our salvation is by grace through faith (Eph 2:4–9), it is nevertheless also the case that we are "created

28. On the history of the "seven deadly sins" in Christian thought, see DeYoung, *Glittering Vices*, 21–38; Okholm, *Dangerous Passions*, 2–6.

29. Cassian, *Conferences*, 1.4.

30. On this topic, see further T. Williams, *Confronting Injustice*.

in Christ Jesus for good works" (Eph 2:10) and that God "has granted to us all things that pertain to life and godliness" (2 Pet 1:3), and therefore we are to "make every effort to supplement [our] faith with virtue" (2 Pet 1:5).[31] As Rebecca Konyndyk DeYoung explains, "Living as a Christian takes discipline and practice, and such activities are not replacing Christ's saving work but rather are enabled by it."[32] Cassian himself comments that "it is impossible for a person to deserve to triumph over a passion before he has understood that he is not able to obtain victory in the struggle by his own diligence and his own effort, even though in order to be cleansed he must always be careful and attentive, day and night."[33] It is, indeed, the grace of God that initiates and sustains all of our efforts. And yet, as the church fathers studied throughout this book have emphasized time and again, our active participation in the process of sanctification is required; there must be real effort on our part (always, of course, in cooperation with the Holy Spirit) if we are to grow in Christ's likeness. Cyril too recognized this basic synergism in the process of sanctification; as he puts it at the end of the "Procatechesis," "For it is in me to speak, in you to purpose, and in God to bring to completion" ("Procat.," §17). Striving for holiness and single-mindedness is, therefore, not in opposition to God's grace but is in fact the right use of the grace that God does give us.

In sum, when we speak of calling our students to a life of disciple-ship and transformation into Christ's likeness, we cannot avoid the charge to turn from sin as a crucial part of taking on the character of Christ. As Christian schools consider their approach to spiritual formation, Cyril helps us to see that we must transcend imparting knowledge or inspiring positive feelings about God. Instead, we must aim at something much greater: at cooperating with the Holy Spirit to assist our students in the difficult and yet eternally significant movement from death to life, training them to recognize and turn away from sin as they increasingly recognize and turn towards virtue and Christ himself. Now that we have a better idea of what spiritual formation is ultimately aiming at, we can begin to develop the foundational structures and strategies that will help our students make forward progress in their spiritual journeys over the course of their time at our institutions.

---

31. See DeYoung, *Glittering Vices*, 28.
32. DeYoung, *Glittering Vices*, 29.
33. Cassian, *Conferences*, 5.14.

PLANNING FOR SPIRITUAL FORMATION

Thankfully, Cyril did not leave his catechumens without a strategy for engaging with the Holy Spirit in this movement from death to life. In the second half of his "Procatechesis" (§9–17), Cyril outlines a basic vision for how spiritual formation can take place. While some of his points necessarily reflect the sacramental context of baptismal preparation,[34] we will find that Cyril's metaphor of constructing a building provides a useful image for stimulating our thinking about the structures that will best assist students in working towards spiritual growth and prepare them within their own souls to "fight the battle of the Lord" ("Procat.," §10). Though the emphasis of this section will be on how Cyril's insights can help us develop an institution-wide plan for spiritual formation, these strategies can be just as relevant for individual teachers seeking to foster spiritual growth in their own classrooms.

Constructing the Building

Cyril does not hide his overarching strategy from his catechumens; rather, he is explicit with them about what is required for their journey to spiritual maturity ("Procat.," §11):

> Consider with me the catechizing to be a building. Unless we dig deeply, and set the foundation, unless we join the structure of the house together with a sequence of chains, that no gaping hole be found, and the building become unsound, there is no benefit from our former work. But it is necessary that stone follow upon stone in sequence, and corner fall into place with corner, and that our excesses be shaved off, so that the finished building may arise. In such a way we are offering you stones, as it were, of wisdom. It is necessary to hear the things concerning the living God. It is necessary to hear the things concerning judgment. It is necessary to hear the things concerning Christ. It is necessary to hear the things concerning the resurrection. And many things are spoken sequentially, which are now being delivered as a seed, but then will be offered as a harmonious whole. But unless you connect them as one, and remember what is first and what is second, the builder might build, but again the building will not have a solid foundation.

34. Here I primarily have in mind Cyril's exhortations that the catechumens receive the exorcisms that were part of the pre-baptismal liturgy of the early church ("Procat.," §9, 13–14). See further Yarnold, *Cyril of Jerusalem*, 37.

In this image, Cyril describes the process of laying a strong foundation as the basis for a building's further construction.[35] As applied to his context, it is his catechetical lectures as part of the catechumen's preparation for baptism that he hopes will serve as a solid foundation for further growth into Christian maturity. To this end, Cyril points out that his sequence of catechetical lectures builds from one topic to the next, providing in sum "a systematic instruction in doctrine," following the basic contours of the Creed.[36] The topics suggested by Cyril in this passage—God, judgment, Christ, resurrection—roughly correspond to our modern schema of creation-fall-redemption-restoration, a sequence of movements within the biblical narrative that follows, logically and sequentially, one to the next. As Cyril is quick to point out, such a strategy must be carefully conceived and executed so that each step of the process leads into the next.[37] What this suggests for us, then, is that not only can we think about faith development stages writ large (purgation-illumination-contemplation), but we can also develop plans for how to help our students progress within the stages themselves.

As educators, we instinctively recognize that our academic curriculum has to be sensitive to our learners' developmental stages as expressed in a clear, aligned sequence through a given course of study. And yet, we are often content with a less intentional approach to spiritual formation. What if, though, we understood spiritual formation to be quite similar to, say, mathematics education? What if, in both instances, we recognized the need to allow both our content and our process to be informed by the present state of our learners' abilities, a clear objective, and a clear plan for moving our learners along to higher levels of understanding?[38] In other words, our efforts at spiritual formation should not be haphazardly throwing different things at kids and seeing what sticks but rather should proceed from a well-considered plan that takes into account both the internal logic of Christian doctrine as well as the developmental needs of our learners. For instance, J. I. Packer and Gary Parrett suggest taking advantage of the great capacity of young children to memorize information that they will be able

35. Cyril's imagery calls to mind Paul's treatment of this theme in Eph 2:19–22. See also the development of this theme in D. Smith and Felch, *Teaching and Christian Imagination*, 139–204.

36. Yarnold, *Cyril of Jerusalem*, 36.

37. Part of the reason for this approach, in Cyril's context, was to make sure that the mysteries of the Christian faith were presented only to those who had demonstrated themselves to be worthy of hearing them ("Procat.," §12). In fact, instruction about the sacraments of baptism and the Lord's Supper was reserved for *after* they were baptized and had partaken of their first Communion. On this so-called *disciplina arcani*, see further Yarnold, *Cyril of Jerusalem*, 49–54.

38. See Packer and Parrett, *Grounded in the Gospel*, 138.

to reflect upon ever more deeply as they progress through their lives: "By seizing upon our children's God-ordained ability to commit verses, creeds, hymns, lists, and much more to memory when they are still very young, we are helping them to 'fill the cupboard' of their souls."[39]

This image of "filling the cupboard" helps us recognize that purity of heart is most likely to come about when positive inputs replace negative ones. In other words, it is not enough to try to avoid corrupting thoughts, words, and deeds, for instead one must actively fill oneself with what is good, beautiful, and true. Cyril makes this point throughout the "Procatechesis." For instance, his exhortation to "let your tongue not speak insignificant words, nor let your sight look at sin, nor let your mind wander toward what is not profitable" ("Procat.," §8) is immediately followed by his directive to "let your feet hurry to the catechetical lectures" ("Procat.," §9). This strategy was, in fact, central to the ancient notion of education as cultivating virtue; we recall, for instance, Chrysostom's injunction to shape students' souls by immersing them in the stories of the Bible,[40] Basil's interest in appropriating pagan literature to give students virtuous deeds to emulate,[41] and Benedict's use of memorization and repetition to imprint the words, images, and cadences of the psalter deeply into his monks' minds.[42] It is again worth pointing out that these strategies can be impactful on all students, not just those who may already be regenerate; meaningful engagement with formative spiritual practices was in fact required of those who were not yet baptized.[43] Here the image of "filling the cupboard" feels particularly apropos: we can help provide our students with the tools that they need for furthering their spiritual development, but it is ultimately up to them, in cooperation with the Holy Spirit, to actually open the cupboard, take these things out, and put them to good use. This approach, therefore, seeks to balance Chrysostom's concern for "guarding the gates" of the student's senses from negative inputs with a perspective that seeks to flood a student with positive inputs that aim to inspire a life of faith and virtue. We are more likely, I suggest, to see students pursue purity of heart when we have placed before them a highly desirable, alternative version of the good life than when we merely condemn

---

39. Packer and Parrett, *Grounded in the Gospel*, 138–39.

40. See again Chrysostom, "Vain.," §39, and ch. 3 above.

41. See again Basil, "YM," §7, and ch. 4 above.

42. See again Benedict, *RB*, §18, and ch. 5 above.

43. See Jensen, *Baptismal Imagery*, 38: "Preparing candidates for baptism also involved rigorous ascetical practices for the purpose of both purifying and strengthening, not only for the rite but also for the life candidates would be expected to live once they were full members of the church."

our culture's false visions without giving them an imagination for a different kind of life and the practices and habits to begin walking in that way.[44]

At this point, we might mistake Cyril for conceiving of catechesis as merely seeking to construct a theological curriculum that appeals to his catechumens' minds alone, as if simply presenting correct information in the correct sequence is sufficient for the making of disciples. This is not, however, Cyril's approach. "Let your mind be refined in the fire toward reverence," Cyril begins, "let your soul be forged as copper, let the hardness of your unbelief be beaten out on the anvil, let the excess scales fall away from the iron, and let the pure remain" ("Procat.," §15). Beyond the intellectual domain of the mind, then, there is a further concern for the soul, as representative of the entire human person. Simply knowing the facts about God is not enough, Cyril insists; in order to resist the wiles of the devil, he tells his catechumens, it is necessary to "prepare your heart" and "pray more frequently," for these things are necessary if they are to rightly receive Cyril's instruction about the heavenly mysteries ("Procat.," §16). Returning at the close of the address to the metaphor of the building, Cyril issues a final exhortation that the building resulting from this catechizing be made of "gold, and silver, and precious stones," rather than of "hay, straw, and chaff" ("Procat.," §17; cf. 1 Cor 3:12–15). To this end, recognizing the role that his own teaching and the Holy Spirit play in this process in addition to his catechumens' own effort, Cyril proclaims, "Let us strengthen our minds. Let us direct our souls. Let us prepare our hearts. Let us run for our soul. Let us hope for eternal things" ("Procat.," §17). Clearly, then, catechesis is not merely a cognitive exercise but seeks to effect change that encompasses the whole human person.[45]

Combining this with the message of the first half of the "Procatechesis," we can conclude that Cyril's approach to catechesis encompasses intellectual, affective, and behavioral components, each of which has a role to play in preparing the catechumen for baptism. In other words, learning right doctrine about God, converting the heart to desire the things of God, and turning away from sin are three strands to the cord of catechesis that cannot be separated if this catechizing is to make a deep and lasting impression. This basic pattern of heads, hearts, and hands is in fact a deeply biblical concept of how spiritual growth happens;[46] these three aspects of the Bible's teaching are summarized, respectively, in the Creed (which teaches us what to believe), the Lord's Prayer (which teaches us how to turn our hearts to

44. See again J. Smith, *Desiring the Kingdom.*
45. On this point, see further Bullis, "Applying St. Cyril's Pedagogy," 363–65.
46. See, e.g., Deut 6:5; Matt 22:36–40; John 14:6; Acts 2:42.

God in worship), and the Ten Commandments or Decalogue (which teaches us how to live ethically).[47] Historically, these three items have been at the heart of the church's catechesis, and continue to function in this capacity in many traditions today.[48] As articulated by Packer and Parrett, these three elements correspond to Jesus's threefold self-revelation in John 14:6 and converge to form the goal of all catechetical work, which is to form people who are "taught by the Truth," "liberated by the Life," and "walk in the Way."[49] And we have, of course, already encountered this threefold pattern in the discussion of curricular throughlines in chapter 4 of this book.

By being attentive to all three of these facets of the faith, we can be confident that we have taken into account the full implications of the gospel for the full human person, thus establishing a "plumb line" for our building that will help ensure that it is "properly vertical" as it is constructed.[50] Such a well-built structure contributes to the formation of the kind of person who, with the help of the God who "has the power to preserve the genuine and to make of the hypocrite a person of faith," will be filled "with the heavenly things of the new covenant" ("Procat.," §17). Drawing upon these insights, we can now begin sketching a blueprint for how to cooperate in a strategic fashion with the work of the Holy Spirit in leading our students from death to life.

Catechesis by Design

Having articulated a clearer understanding of how spiritual formation works, it is now possible to explore a practical approach to guiding students on this path in a way that is sensitive to both the Christian tradition and our present learners. Like Cyril, we can undertake the work of catechizing our students, not haphazardly but by design in light of our overarching objectives. Generating such an intentional and rightly sequenced program for spiritual formation will, no doubt, require the cooperation of both administrators who are charged with articulating, aligning, and safeguarding the design as well as individual teachers who know what role they are to play in helping execute the plan. To be maximally effective, designing an institutional program of catechesis cannot be the exclusive domain of Bible teachers or chapel coordinators; while some elements may indeed be closely tied to particular contexts such as those, the argument of this book has been that teaching for spiritual formation is a calling for *all* Christian educators, a

47. See further Packer and Parrett, *Grounded in the Gospel*, 117–30.

48. See, e.g., Packer and Scandrett, *To Be a Christian*.

49. Packer and Parrett, *Grounded in the Gospel*, 91; cf. 130–36.

50. Packer and Parrett, *Grounded in the Gospel*, 118.

point which will continue to be underscored in the following section. While we cannot guarantee any particular spiritual outcomes in our students, we can at least be confident that we have pursued these aims with the same level of thoughtfulness and intentionality as we did any other part of their education.

In our attempts to do "catechesis by design," we would do well to give careful attention to the following three stages of the design process: the identification of a set of desired outcomes or aims; the selection of pedagogical strategies that take into account what is appropriate for students' spiritual, intellectual, and emotional levels of development; and the use of quality resources to support the work. Each of these three elements—outcomes, strategy, and resources—will now be considered in turn.

First, we can identify what intellectual, affective, and behavioral outcomes pertaining to spiritual formation are appropriate for our learners at different stages of their development. It is perhaps easiest to work backwards from our aspirations for our graduates. What do we want them to know? How do we want them to be able to engage with God? How do we want them to be able to relate to others? The idea of biblical throughlines, described in chapter 4 above, may provide one way of articulating such an aspirational portrait of the Christian life. In this section, however, I want to illustrate an approach to catechetical design through the lens of one particular desired student outcome that will closely resonate with the contemplative themes that have coursed through this book: the cultivation of the habits of a life of prayer. While I would consider this to be an outcome that primarily falls within the affective domain, insofar as prayer is a devotional practice that directs the inner gaze of our hearts toward God, it is nevertheless the case that there are intellectual and behavioral aspects involved in learning to pray. Perhaps, then, I could sketch out a set of aspirational outcomes with respect to prayer as follows:

Heads	Hearts	Hands
Students will be able to articulate a basic theology of prayer and be able to describe major forms of prayer rooted in the Christian tradition.	Students will be able to engage with and reflect upon different forms of prayer as a personal devotional practice.	Students will be able to pray out loud for others and to lead others in prayer at appropriate times and places.

With this set of aspirational outcomes in place, we can now construct a sequence of formative experiences that could lead students to grow towards this goal. The next step, then, would be to identify specific benchmarks for which different classroom teachers would be responsible. For the purposes of this illustration, I will focus on a potential first set of benchmarks designed to work towards the established set of desired outcomes, setting out what benchmarks our students should have achieved in this area as early elementary students:

Heads	Hearts	Hands
Students will be able to articulate a basic theology of prayer and be able to describe major forms of prayer rooted in the Christian tradition. STEP 1 (Early Elementary) **Benchmark**: Students will be able to recite the Lord's Prayer and answer basic questions about prayer.	Students will be able to engage with and reflect upon different forms of prayer as a personal devotional practice. STEP 1 (Early Elementary) **Benchmark**: Students will be able to participate in imaginative prayer exercises.	Students will be able to pray out loud for others and to lead others in prayer at appropriate times and places. STEP 1 (Early Elementary) **Benchmark**: Students will be able to lead the class in prayer before lunch or snack.

The first of these benchmarks follows from the Lord's response to his disciples when they asked him to teach them to pray (Luke 11:1–4). Indeed, the Lord's Prayer has, historically speaking, been the cornerstone of the Christian life of prayer, revealing to us Christ himself, as "each petition is a window into Jesus' own life of prayer—His reliance on and manifestation of the One He called Father."[51] Early elementary students should certainly know this prayer (if they do not already) and, more generally, have a rudimentary theology of prayer that can serve as a foundation for their further engagement with prayer in future years. The second benchmark proceeds from the recognition that a significant means of connecting with Jesus involves the use of the imagination, a point which recalls our discussion of *lectio divina* and the prayer of Examen in chapter 2 of this book. This benchmark, then, is designed to help introduce even very young students to the contemplative stream of Christian spirituality, such that they have the opportunity not just to know about God but to experience God at a heart level.[52] The third of these benchmarks aims to develop in students the embodied practice of slowing down and thanking God, who is the source of all our sustenance, both physical and spiritual, before each meal.[53] Following the precedent of

51. Hill, *Lord's Prayer*, 4.

52. See Boyd, *Imaginative Prayer*, 13–23.

53. This benchmark also has the added and practical benefit of helping students practice speaking in public, perhaps tying into other desired student learning outcomes.

ancient Judaism, it has been customary for Christians over the centuries to say a blessing prior to a meal, as this formative practice "reminds us that we should give thanks to God who is the giver of everything" and serves to "help bring families, friends, and communities together in gratitude and thanksgiving to God, thus making a profound connection with God and one another."[54] These specific benchmarks may not be appropriate for every institution of Christian education, as they merely reflect one possible theological and institutional context, but should serve as a sufficient example for the kinds of benchmarks that schools could develop for their own needs. In any event, clear and carefully sequenced benchmarks provide a clear target towards which schools and teachers can aim, making possible attempts to measure and reflect on the extent to which the desired learning outcomes are being achieved.[55]

Second, we can plan appropriate pedagogical strategies that will effectively engage students with these ideas and practices. As with any other subject of study, we will need to consider a pedagogical approach that will resonate with the developmental level of our learners. Beyond this, however, as explicitly Christian educators, we can take into account the insights regarding community life, classroom management, and the use of time and space discussed in the previous chapter of this book. As for the first of the above benchmarks, we want to take advantage of early elementary students' innate capacity for memorization such that the students commit to memory some foundational facts about prayer. Likewise, with respect to the second benchmark, we want to take advantage of the ability of younger children to engage their imaginations to put themselves in various evocative stories or scenes, as well as to draw on the wisdom and relational capital of their teachers to lead them through these exercises in a slow and prayerful way. For the third of these benchmarks, we can again draw on students' capacities for memorization and imitation to establish a classroom "liturgy" before mealtime that students will eventually be able to reproduce and take ownership of themselves. Thus, we may articulate our strategies for achieving these benchmarks as follows:

54. Bevins and Bevins, *Field Guide*, 18.

55. This point may be particularly useful for schools that have accreditation requirements to track the spiritual development of the student body.

Heads	Hearts	Hands
Students will be able to articulate a basic theology of prayer and be able to describe major forms of prayer rooted in the Christian tradition. STEP 1 (Early Elementary) **Benchmark**: Students will be able to recite the Lord's Prayer and answer basic questions about prayer. **Strategy**: The teacher works with students to memorize the Lord's Prayer line by line before then assisting them in memorizing a series of answers to a given set of questions about prayer.	Students will be able to engage with and reflect upon different forms of prayer as a personal devotional practice. STEP 1 (Early Elementary) **Benchmark**: Students will be able to participate in imaginative prayer exercises. **Strategy**: The teacher leads students through guided imaginative prayer exercises by reading aloud the material and prompts, following up with discussion questions or conversation starters.	Students will be able to pray out loud for others and to lead others in prayer at appropriate times and places. STEP 1 (Early Elementary) **Benchmark**: Students will be able to lead the class in prayer before lunch or snack. **Strategy**: The teacher models leading the class in prayer before lunch by praying the same prayer every day until students have memorized it; students will then take turns praying it every day.

These are certainly not the only ways we could achieve these benchmarks, but they do have the advantage of being both specific and actionable. There is, again, opportunity for further creativity on the part of the individual teacher; perhaps hand motions or songs would be helpful for enabling very young students to memorize some of this material. The role of the teacher is also quite pronounced in the second benchmark; the fact that we cannot simply throw our young students into the deep waters of contemplative prayer means that we will need a carefully planned, teacher-driven approach in which the teacher walks through every step of the experience alongside her students. Note, too, how the strategy selected for each benchmark is merely one out of a greater possible list of options. For instance, with the third benchmark, we could have had the teacher model spontaneous prayers of thanksgiving prior to mealtime and eventually shift this role to different students. In adopting the strategy described above, however, we are applying the insights about the formative effects of meaningful memorization that we described in the previous chapter of this book, seeking to help expand our students' imagination for prayer and increase their vocabulary and fluency in the patterns and rhythms of Christian prayer.

Third, we can select the appropriate resources that will assist teachers in executing these strategies. As with the above steps, there are no "right" choices here, insofar as different denominational or cultural contexts might wish to make use of different resources. The point, though, is that quality resources do exist and have the potential to support individual teachers who may not feel qualified enough or who may lack the time to create their own resources. Thus, I have selected the catechism *To Be a Christian* to help provide students with basic facts concerning the how, what, why, and when of prayer.[56] For the second benchmark, I have chosen the exercises printed in Jared Patrick Boyd's book *Imaginative Prayer*, aiming to work through the first part, on "God's Love," over the course of the semester if a teacher does this exercise with her students once every three weeks or so.[57] For the third benchmark, having sampled some of the options printed in Winfield and Kay Bevins' wonderful little *Field Guide for Family Prayer*, I have selected an early Methodist prayer for these young students to memorize and recite before mealtimes.[58] To the extent that school administrators and instructional leaders can help supply their faculty with quality, appropriate resources for achieving these benchmarks, teachers will likely feel much better equipped to carry out this work with confidence. My plan for helping students meet these benchmarks is now complete:

---

56. See Packer and Scandrett, *To Be a Christian*, 66–67.

57. Boyd, *Imaginative Prayer*, 33–72.

58. Bevins and Bevins, *Field Guide*, 20. See also the extensive age-appropriate collection of table prayers in Wigger, *Together We Pray*, 9–46.

Heads	Hearts	Hands
Students will be able to articulate a basic theology of prayer and be able to describe major forms of prayer rooted in the Christian tradition. STEP 1 (Early Elementary) **Benchmark**: Students will be able to recite the Lord's Prayer and answer basic questions about prayer. **Strategy**: The teacher works with students to memorize the Lord's Prayer line by line before then assisting them in memorizing a series of answers to a given set of questions about prayer. **Resource**: J. I. Packer and Joel Scandrett, *To Be a Christian*, catechism questions #154–59.	Students will be able to engage with and reflect upon different forms of prayer as a personal devotional practice. STEP 1 (Early Elementary) **Benchmark**: Students will be able to participate in imaginative prayer exercises. **Strategy**: The teacher leads students through guided imaginative prayer exercises by reading aloud the material and prompts, following up with discussion questions or conversation starters. **Resource**: Jared Patrick Boyd, *Imaginative Prayer*, exercises 1–6.	Students will be able to pray out loud for others and to lead others in prayer at appropriate times and places. STEP 1 (Early Elementary) **Benchmark**: Students will be able to lead the class in prayer before lunch or snack. **Strategy**: The teacher models leading the class in prayer before lunch by praying the same prayer every day until students have memorized it; students will then take turns praying it every day. **Resource**: An early Methodist prayer, "Be present at our table, Lord . . ."

If our goal is to use the habits of prayer to expand our students' imaginations, not just for prayer but for the Christian life more generally, these three benchmarks should work well towards this end. The choices of resources, then, was deliberate and strategic. The catechism *To Be a Christian* combines theological precision with an accessible, straightforward style and could be used throughout the entirety of a student's time at the school. Likewise, the exercises in *Imaginative Prayer* are designed to help students form a vision for prayer that encompasses the experience of God, introducing a more contemplative and personal aspect to their understanding of prayer. By focusing on the theme of God's love for them, we hope to root this truth deep into their hearts at an early age. I selected this Methodist prayer, sometimes attributed to John Wesley, because it emphasizes Christ's presence with us at all time and in all places ("Be present at our table, Lord; / Be here and everywhere adored") and uses the imagery of the meal to point forward to the eschatological wedding supper of the Lamb ("Thy people bless, and grant that we / May feast in paradise with Thee"; cf. Rev 19:6–9).[59] With accompanying explanation from the teacher, this prayer is a resource that can help even our youngest learners catch a vision of the Christian life as union with Christ. This prayer can help them even at this early age to frame the Christian life not as moralistic therapeutic deism or as a get-out-of-hell-free pass but rather as a journey by which we grow into ever increasing communion with our Lord, Savior, and King. It is, I believe, the kind of *telos* that can motivate and sustain a lifelong walk with Christ. Different students might connect with each of the elements of this plan differently, but we can trust that the Holy Spirit will meet them, wherever they are in their spiritual journeys, through their engagement with these formative experiences.

One advantage of a carefully designed approach to spiritual formation such as this is that it allows for an institutional posture of continuous reflection and evaluation. Schools can, for instance, measure if a given benchmark is being met, or not. This reminds us of the need to design benchmarks that are actually measurable. It is possible to determine, for instance, if a student has memorized and is able to recite the Methodist prayer before mealtime, but we cannot ultimately judge the heart posture behind such a prayer. Nevertheless, having a clearly defined set of desired learning outcomes means that we can revise our benchmarks, strategies, and curriculum if we sense that one or more of these aspects is not contributing to the broader goal of forming heads, hearts, and hands in accordance with that learning outcome. While the fruit of the seeds we are planting may not be evident for years or even decades to come, we would be wise to be prayerfully attuned to the extent to which changing contexts and different groups of learners may require adjustments to our plans.

Another advantage of this kind of approach is that all teachers can contribute meaningful and relevant ways of engaging students in this sequence of formative experiences. A high school English teacher, for instance, could include a formal study of prayers (e.g., those of John Donne) in a unit on poetry. A foreign language teacher, moreover, could design activities in which students practice praying in the foreign language, either for the needs of one another or perhaps even for the people in the target culture. A choral teacher could train her students to sing classical arrangements of prayers in the Christian tradition (traditional Gregorian chant might be one place to start). A Bible teacher working through the New Testament could assign students reflective journals in which they record their engagement with select portions of the Gospels through the practice of *lectio divina*.[60]

---

59. See Cyril's discussion of this theme in "Procat.," §6.
60. See the development of this point in Bullis, "Applying St. Cyril's Pedagogy," 370–71.

With an expanded imagination for the kinds of formative experiences that could reinforce the institution's catechetical design, the possibilities for engagement across grade levels or subject areas are limitless.

Of course, we must recognize that successfully following a plan such as this will not mechanistically produce or guarantee the desired spiritual outcomes in our learners. We are called to plant and water the seeds, but ultimately it is God who gives the growth (1 Cor 3:5–7). Still, as with every other educational initiative, having a plan is far more likely to "stock the shelves" than throwing random items into the cupboard and seeing where they land. Thus, I have suggested in this section that small, intentional strategic choices to identify age-appropriate benchmarks, consider the most effective pedagogy, and take advantage of the strongest resources can contribute to a larger strategy for providing opportunities for our students to engage the Holy Spirit with their heads, hearts, and hands. In so doing, we can at least feel confident that we are planning for students' spiritual growth with the same effort and intentionality as we are for any other aspect of their development. To return to the metaphors we have explored earlier in this chapter, it will be up to them to one day open their spiritual cupboards or build on these foundations, but we have done all we can to ensure their cupboards are rightly stocked and that the building of their lives rises from a straight and true foundation. And, to return to Cyril, we are engaging in the work of catechesis—designing learning experiences that engage heads, hearts, and hands such that our students have the opportunities to be formed ever more into Christ's likeness, increasingly able to turn away from sin and towards virtue.

FORMATION, REIMAGINED

In this chapter, we have reimagined what we mean by spiritual formation and how we can best partner with the Holy Spirit in moving our students forward on their spiritual journeys. We have taken our inspiration from Cyril of Jerusalem, whose careful catechetical design provided his catechumens with a solid foundation for progress in the Christian life across their intellectual, affective, and behavioral domains. Practically, Cyril helped us see that the first and most foundational movement of the Christian life is the movement from sin to virtue; even those with little or no genuine interest in the Christian faith, Cyril argued, should receive an invitation to the Christian way of life and training in its practices. With this in mind, we then examined how engaging students' heads, hearts, and hands through a strategic process of establishing benchmarks, choosing appropriate pedagogy, and selecting quality resources can provide opportunities for students to encounter the Holy Spirit. Having reached the conclusion of our journey through the church fathers' insights on teaching and learning, we now have left only to synthesize how we as educators might apply the findings of this book through the lens of a "Teacher's Rule of Life."

7

Conclusion

A Teacher's Rule of Life

In this book, we have engaged the writings of the church fathers for the purpose of helping us reimagine various aspects of Christian education and consider the practices by which we could realize these insights in the classroom. It is fitting, therefore, that in this conclusion we will consider one last historic Christian practice of spiritual formation that will allow us to synthesize what we have learned in this book into an actionable and applicable plan for revitalizing the work of Christian education. One of the most important tools for undertaking the work of spiritual formation is what is often called a Rule of Life, which takes its name from the monastic rules that governed the lives of monks in different communities (for instance, the *Rule* of Saint Benedict). As generally understood, a personal Rule of Life is an intentional pattern of personal commitments and spiritual disciplines that, taken together, provides structure and direction for journeying through life in a thoughtful and strategic manner.[1] We can think of it functioning akin to both a map, charting a course for the journey ahead, as well as a compass, helping us to get back on track when we wander away from the path. A comprehensive personal Rule of Life might, for instance, cover a wide range of spiritual, relational, physical, financial, and missional priorities that

---

1. See further Macchia, *Crafting a Rule of Life*, 14–15; Scazzero, *Emotionally Healthy Spirituality*, 189–206.

reflect our unique roles, gifts, desires, and aspirations.[2] While commending the process of developing a personal Rule of Life in its entirety, in concluding this book I would like to turn our focus to something more narrowly targeted for the audience of this book, which I am calling a "Teacher's Rule of Life." While many educators are no doubt familiar with the process of crafting a personal philosophy of education, this exercise aims to provide stimuli that can integrate faith into such a philosophy in a more consistent and meaningful way per the content of this book.

As you work through this chapter, please pause at the indicated points, reflect on the given questions, and record your responses (a worksheet is included as an appendix to this book if you would like to make use of it). If possible, you may wish to reflect on your responses with a trusted friend or colleague who can help provide an outside perspective on your life and work.

CREATING YOUR TEACHER'S RULE OF LIFE

This exercise is designed to lead you into deeper reflection on your own vocation as a Christian educator and the commitments and habits that will help you to flourish in your role. While we will draw upon the major movements and themes of this book as an organizing structure for this reflection, you will get the most out of this process if the Rule you develop is both individualized and realistic. Given that each Christian educator is unique, with a different background, set of life experiences, personality, and strengths and weaknesses, there can be no "one size fits all" Teacher's Rule of Life. Likewise, an idealized Rule that cannot actually be followed, given personal or institutional limitations, is a certain recipe for disillusionment and frustration. With these guidelines in mind, we can now turn to the process of developing a Rule, beginning in the same place as this book by bringing into focus a sharper image of our own identities as teachers.

The Teacher

For those called to a career in Christian education, the specters of discouragement, burnout, and cynicism always loom large. With the help of Gregory the Great, however, we explored how engagement in contemplative practices can foster a rich interior life sufficient for the work at hand. The

---

2. See further the discussion of each of these areas in Macchia, *Crafting a Rule of Life*, 21–134.

great enemy is, of course, our culture of hurried, frantic busyness; it will take conscious commitments, then, just as it did in Gregory's time, to step back and tend to our own lives with God. Operating on the principle of "you cannot give away what you do not have," it will always be the overflow of our own spiritual lives that has the best potential to authentically invite students into this alternative way of life.

As you begin your Teacher's Rule of Life, then, start by identifying the foundational contemplative practices that will ground your days and keep God ever before your mind. While earlier in this book I commended the habits of reflecting through the prayer of Examen, meditating on the Bible through *lectio divina*, and finding a "soul friend" for the sake of mutual encouragement and edification, what matters most is finding the rhythms and practices that will contribute to the building up of your own spiritual life. What practices, then, will serve as the foundation for your own life with God? Even something as simple as listening to a recording of the morning office from the *Book of Common Prayer* on the way to work can be a relatively painless way of beginning to incorporate these kinds of practices into your day. Your Teacher's Rule of Life starts here because it is these habits that matter most, for they will endure even if you change jobs or retire from teaching altogether. To again reiterate, our own spiritual formation matters because greater communion with God is not simply a prerequisite for our work but the very *telos* of our lives.

This section should also include your own understanding of your individual calling to be a Christian educator. *What made you want to be a teacher? What do you have to offer your students and colleagues? How would you define a "successful" career?* Gregory challenged us to see ourselves as physicians of the soul, prayerfully discerning how to make the most of every opportunity to encourage our students on their spiritual journeys and to point them to the God who alone can bind their wounds and heal their brokenness. Having a clear and compelling understanding of your own call to the work of Christian education can help guide and sustain a career that will inevitably have its share of disappointments and distractions; coming back to this statement (and perhaps revising it over time as necessary) can therefore serve as an important means of encouragement to persevere in your work.

The Student

The next section of the Teacher's Rule of Life offers opportunities to reflect on the students to whom you are called to teach. In light of John

Chrysostom's homily "On Vainglory," we considered how our learners are complex, embodied persons who have suffered the corrupting effects of sin and now need a transformative personal encounter with God. As teachers, we have the profound and weighty responsibility of helping point our students to Christ. As Chrysostom demonstrated, this kind of education will go beyond imparting information or building skills to encompass the work of forming our students' souls, a task that requires specific attention to the various sensory inputs that are forming our students' inner lives.

Your Teacher's Rule of Life, then, should next include a description of your sense of the particular needs of the learners with whom you work. For Chrysostom, it was vainglory that was the primary vice that needed to be rooted out of young people, but perhaps your observations of your students will lead you to identify a different set of symptoms demonstrating their need for Christ. *How are you engaging the full range of your students' senses in order to lead them towards what is good, beautiful, and true? What corrupting things are you presently letting pass through your students' "gates"? Where does your teaching need to take more seriously the fully embodied nature of your learners?*

This section should also include a set of commitments related to your understanding of the teacher-student relationship. I argued that meeting the needs of our students has less to do with being our students' friends and more to do with incarnating a non-anxious presence that is prayerfully open and present to our students. Only by taking the time to listen to what is truly going on in their inner selves, by demonstrating ourselves to be trustworthy and compassionate adults, can we hope to have the spiritual influence that we so desire. How, then, do you aim to go about this? How do you make yourself available, accessible, and relatable to your students in a way that students would feel comfortable bringing their concerns and struggles to you? Try intentionally committing to certain forms of student engagement, even if it is as simple as consistently showing up for a certain sport or activity, and see what doors the Lord opens through that avenue.

Curriculum

The Teacher's Rule of Life next considers in detail the actual content of what you teach. Our study of Basil of Caesarea's "Address to Young Men" helped us see that our curriculum has the potential to have a significant influence on our students' understanding of and desire to pursue a life of virtue. Like Chrysostom, Basil recognized the deeply formative nature of everything that our students are taking in. While Basil likewise identified the need to

carefully guard our students from exposure to certain things, he nevertheless clearly articulated the principle that "all truth is God's truth," meaning that he could confidently engage his students with all that was good,
beautiful, and true from pagan literature. In the same way, then, we have the
opportunity to reflect on how our curriculum, regardless of what discipline
or level we teach, can point students towards Christian virtue.

For this section of your Teacher's Rule of Life, consider the subject
matter that you teach. *Where does your curriculum allow for opportunities to
invite students into a life of virtue? Are students being inspired and exhorted
towards virtuous actions? How could your curriculum train students in these
virtues so that they come to live them out?* While I argued that an emphasis
on cultivating virtue can serve as an overarching framework connecting all
disciplines in pursuit of a common aim, it nevertheless remains the work of
individual teachers to connect their specific subject matter with this unifying theme in a way that is authentically grounded in their curriculum and
responsive to the observed needs of the students that are being taught. Here
it may be helpful to identify and commit to working towards one specific
virtue or aspect of Christian identity through your curriculum. Whether
this is conceived of through the lens of an essential question, a biblical
throughline, or some other curricular paradigm, this provides the foundation for then designing learning experiences that will bridge the curricular
goals to actual unit or lesson plans. Given that we want students not just
to understand virtue on an intellectual level but to be inspired to pursue it
and actually have opportunities to put it into practice, these learning experiences should ideally engage students' heads, hearts, and hands. Which
virtue, then, could you structure your course around, and how could you
help your students engage with this virtue? By carefully reflecting on how to
use your curriculum to inculcate a selected virtue in your students, they will
increasingly catch a vision for how to grow as virtuous followers of Christ.

Pedagogy

The next section of the Teacher's Rule of Life focuses on the pedagogical
commitments that drive your actual classroom instruction. As we observed
in the *Rule* of Saint Benedict, how we go about the work of teaching and
learning is just as important in forming our students as is the content of
the class itself. Part of the genius of Benedict's approach to the monastic life
was that he gave careful attention to the rhythms and routines that would
shape the lives of his monks ever more into Christ's likeness. In so doing,
Benedict's monks could experience the formative power of the Christian

life as fully embodied persons shaped by community life, time, and space, allowing for the transformation of their heads, hearts, and hands. Likewise, our thoughtful reflection on our pedagogical practices has the potential to move our students forward in their spiritual lives.

As you begin this section, think about the kind of classroom culture that would reflect Christian ideals and the practices that could promote such a shared environment. *What kind of classroom commitments would you and your students need to make to another? How can you design learning experiences that encourage students to build up one another in love? How can you forge unity among your students?* Through careful attention to questions such as these, it is possible to give concrete shape to a vision of a learning community characterized by faith, hope, and love. Of course, protecting the integrity of such a classroom culture will also require consideration of matters of classroom management or discipline, providing still another opportunity for reflection on how even this aspect of classroom life can point students towards Christ.

This section of your Rule should also set out some of your core convictions related to your use of time and space. Benedict rightly saw that it was essential to establish daily rhythms that could promote order, balance, and spiritual growth in his monks; in the same way, we can make intentional use of time through strategies such as beginning each class with a set liturgy, engaging with the church calendar, and creating space for reflection, silence, and stillness. How, then, can you use time to reinforce a Christian vision of the good life? Moreover, Benedict identified the arrangement of physical space and the use of things therein as additional avenues of formative engagement, challenging us to reflect on if we are making intentional choices about our use of space to develop virtue and foster community. Similarly, then, how can you use space in a way that feels distinctively Christian? In creating a classroom culture reinforced by a careful approach to the use of time and space, students will not just hear about a different way of life but actually be able to experience it for themselves.

Formation

Finally, your Teacher's Rule of Life sets out your plans for how you can collaborate with others to craft an overall strategy that works towards a clear and consistent vision of spiritual growth for students at your institution. This requires, first of all, a right understanding of the goal of the Christian life and the stages by which we mature. As Cyril of Jerusalem's "Procatechesis" explained, the initial movement of the spiritual life by which we will ultimately come to contemplate God is the movement from death to life; this requires, then, the hard work of turning away from sin and death and towards virtue and new life in Christ. With this aim in mind, Cyril evidenced a concern to make use of a sequenced and strategic plan that took seriously the intellectual, affective, and behavioral domains of the human person. Cyril therefore challenged our institutions to be just as intentional in their overall approach to students' spiritual formation as they are with any other aspect of their education.

Ideally, this section should involve identifying your institution's set of aspirational learning goals with respect to spiritual formation and describing how your efforts align with those of other educators in your institution to assist students in working towards those goals. I suspect, however, that most Christian schools have not explicitly defined these desired learning outcomes. This section, then, may in fact provide an initial opportunity to cast a vision for your institution in this regard. Gather a group of interested people at your institution and start setting out possible benchmarks pertaining to spiritual formation, the pedagogical strategies that will best support your learners in growing towards these aims, and the best resources that can facilitate this work. Careful consideration should be given to relevant aspects of your institution's denominational or theological identity, which may provide a starting point for considering some of these outcomes.

The important point to note here is that, regardless of the extent to which your institution has an explicit understanding of its goals for student spiritual formation, Cyril's call to create a strategic, sequenced approach to catechesis cannot be realized by working in isolation. Conversations with colleagues and administrators are, therefore, essential to ensure proper alignment and to confirm that you are not working at cross-purposes with the efforts of others. Do not underestimate the power of what the Spirit can accomplish through even a small group of educators who collaborate in such an important work!

When you have completed your Rule, share it with a colleague, friend, or your spouse. Frame it on your desk as a reminder of who you are, who your students are, and why, how, and to what end you teach. And while you will no doubt never fully reach the destination and perfectly accomplish all that you have set out to do, may you enjoy the adventure of continuing to make the vision of Christian teaching and learning that you set out in your Rule ever more a reality for your students.

A REFLECTION ON THE JOURNEY

This book opened with the claim that our convulsed age demands an approach to Christian education capable of responding to the complexities and challenges of our present time and place. The vision of Christian education set forth in this book has drawn on the wisdom of our great forefathers in the faith, whose writings have challenged us to reimagine various aspects of our vocation. In my own journey through the writings of the church fathers, I have been consistently struck by the confidence and boldness with which they set forth their vision of the Christian life. In both their willingness to drink deeply from the well of Scripture and their ability to carefully discern the signs of the times, the church fathers still manage to startle, delight, and convict us even today.

Perhaps, then, what the church fathers can most offer Christian educators today is a call to take heart and have courage. While we must acknowledge and take seriously the institutional, societal, and theological obstacles to the vision of Christian education advanced in this book, much less the convulsions that continue to remind us that we live in a broken and fallen world, we can and must remember that we worship a God who is constant and unchanging in his purposes. "In the world you will have tribulation," Jesus told his disciples. "But take heart; I have overcome the world" (John 16:33). May we, like those who have gone before us, rise to the challenge of our times, faithfully and fearlessly passing down to our students the way of new life in Christ, rejoicing to hear them take up the cry that has resounded across the generations: "Glory be to the Father, and to the Son, and to the Holy Spirit, as it was in the beginning, is now, and ever shall be, world without end. Amen."

Appendix 1

Worksheet for Developing Your Teacher's Rule of Life

This worksheet, which adapts the questions from chapter 7 of this book into a more streamlined format, can be used as you begin to craft your own Teacher's Rule of Life.

THE TEACHER

What made you want to be a teacher?

> I loved school
> + all my teachers

What do you have to offer your students and colleagues?

> Christian worldview || life experience - wisdom
> if not intellect

How would you define a "successful" career?

> faithfulness

What spiritual practices will serve as the foundation for your own life with God?

> Church attendance
> prayer | bible

THE STUDENT

How are you engaging the full range of your students' senses in order to lead them towards what is good, beautiful, and true?

Reading + writing + speaking

What corrupting things are you presently letting pass through your students' "gates"?

Where does your teaching need to take more seriously the fully embodied nature of your learners?

More of them, less of me

How do you make yourself available, accessible, and relatable to your students in a way that they would feel comfortable bringing their concerns and struggles to you?

Somehow they know I love them + they love me too

CURRICULUM

Where does your curriculum allow for opportunities to invite students into a life of virtue?

all of our lit does that either by good example or bad

Are students being inspired and exhorted towards virtuous actions?

yes

How could your curriculum train students in these virtues so that they come to live them out?

discussion
encouragement

Is there a particular virtue that you could structure your course around, and how could you help your students engage with that virtue?

Selflessness in a Self-centered
world

PEDAGOGY

What kind of classroom culture do you wish to cultivate?

a Structured one

How can you design learning experiences that encourage students to build up one another in love and forge unity among your students?

How can you use time to reinforce a Christian vision of the good life?

How can you use space in a way that feels distinctively Christian?

FORMATION

What is your institution's understanding of the goal of the Christian life and the stages by which we mature?

How does your institution seek to engage students in the process of spiritual formation?

Does your institution have a denominational or theological identity that can help shape its perspective on spiritual formation?

How can you collaborate with others to refine an overall strategy that works towards a clear and consistent vision of spiritual growth for students?

Appendix 2

Worksheet for Institutional Planning
for Spiritual Formation

This worksheet presents the topics covered in this book as a series of diagnostic questions that school administrators can use in reflecting on their current approach to spiritual formation or in developing new institutional plans around the theme of spiritual formation. Administrators will want to consider answering these questions not only through the lens of classroom instruction, but also on the basis of other aspects of the school's mission and programming (e.g., athletics, admissions, marketing, etc.). In answering each of these questions, it is important to consider not only the messages that are explicitly being sent, but also those that are implicit.

FORMING THE FORMERS

How are we equipping our teachers (and staff, coaches, etc.) to carry out the work of spiritual formation?

How could we go about intentionally nourishing and investing in the spiritual lives of the employees who are on the front lines of delivering our mission with respect to spiritual formation?

Are we providing adequate training for current employees and sufficient onboarding for new employees in this area?

TIME

How does our institution's use of time contribute to the work of spiritual formation?

How can we incorporate more consistent, frequent, and meaningful spiritually formative experiences into our students' daily (and not just weekly, e.g., chapel) experiences?

Are there ways to make connections to the liturgical year?

SPACE

How does our institution's use of space contribute to the work of spiritual formation?

How can we incorporate into our campus areas where students, faculty, and staff can have a quiet, set-aside place for prayer and reflection?

FORMATION

How are we forming our students with respect to Christian doctrines and teachings (head)?

How are we forming them with respect to prayer, the devotional reading of Scripture, and the historic spiritual disciplines of the Christian faith (heart)?

How are we forming them with respect to Christian morality and ethics (hands)?

COMMUNITY

How does our approach to spiritual formation relate to the work of the church and the home?

Can we develop an approach to spiritual formation that is not anti-denominational but rather inclusive of various church traditions, exposing students to a wide range of ways of being Christian?

Can we engage our parent community with opportunities to learn more about the work of spiritual formation, and how they can carry this work into their homes?

Appendix 3

Vision Statement for Spiritual Formation

In introducing a school community to the necessity of teaching for spiritual formation, it may be helpful to set the topic in a broader context. This sample vision statement for spiritual formation, created for Whitefield Academy in Smyrna, Georgia, serves as an example of how this topic can be communicated to a broad audience of stakeholders within the school.

We as human beings have been created in God's image, made to glorify him and to be in relationship with him. When sin entered the world, our very nature was corrupted, our affections were disordered, and our relationship with God was severed. As a result, each one of us walks in the way of death, guilty before God and worthy of judgment. However, through Christ, God has reconciled to himself those who respond to Christ's atoning sacrifice with repentance and faith, granting them forgiveness of sins, union with him in Christ, adoption into his family, and citizenship in his kingdom. Now, by the power of the Holy Spirit, God seeks to lead his people from captivity to sin, transforming us into the image of Jesus Christ and thereby preparing us to be with him for all of eternity.

This Spirit-led process of transformation by which a person grows into Christ's likeness is what we mean by the term "spiritual formation." As a Christ-centered college preparatory school, we desire to partner with Christian families and churches in helping our students encounter the transforming power of the Spirit of the living and active Jesus. As such, our plan for spiritual formation means that we want our students not just to study Christianity, but also to pursue moral progress, cultivate virtue, and imitate Christ in thought, word, and deed. Given our desire to equip students to go on to college and life with a passion for the living and active Jesus, we aim to help students grow into Christ's likeness by expanding their imaginations for a vision of the good life centered on Christ and his kingdom, as well as engaging them with the practices that will embed this vision into their heads, hearts, and hands.

Only such a holistic approach is adequate for meeting the demands of the times in which we live. Given the counter-formational pressures being directed at all of us, and especially at young people, a robust approach to spiritual formation must aim at something more than helping improve our self-esteem and happiness as we otherwise continue along with our lives as planned. Rather, the call to become more like Christ means that we, too, must learn to deny ourselves, take up our crosses, and follow him (Mark 8:34), growing into a way of life characterized by repentance, sacrifice, and self-denial, as well as joy, peace, and intimacy with God. We are, in other words, inviting students into an entirely different way of being human and as such must engage with the entirety of the human person.

Appendix 4

Foundational Principles for Spiritual Formation

While the scope of the work of spiritual formation can feel overwhelming, these clarifications in the forms of guiding principles may help to ease concerns that some members of your school community might have regarding the intersection of spiritual formation and Christian schooling.

Spiritual formation is a process.

Seeing as no one will be fully formed into the image of Christ in this life, we can be sure that none of our students will have "arrived" by the time they graduate from school. Still, by the power of the Holy Spirit, a level of transformation can be experienced during these particularly formative years that has the potential to more fully develop throughout college and life beyond school.

Spiritual formation is for everyone.

Regardless of students' places on their individual spiritual journeys, what church they attend, or what grade they are in, engaging in the shared practices of the historic Christian faith can point students' heads, hearts, and hands to Christ and give them the imagination and the tools to grow in their faith.

Spiritual formation requires partnership.

While the church and the home should be the primary drivers of a child's spiritual formation, the sheer number of hours a student spends at school means that the school also plays a significant role in a child's spiritual development. A Christian school should seek to partner with parents and pastors to collectively help our students journey towards Christ's likeness.

Spiritual formation transforms the whole person.

Because human beings are created as more than just "brains on a stick," spiritual formation transcends the idea of merely teaching a "biblical worldview" in order to engage students' hearts and promote practices by which the Christian way of life can go deep into their innermost being and then out through their actions.

Spiritual formation benefits from intentional planning.

Like any other aspect of a child's education, engaging in the work of spiritual formation well requires an intentional approach that follows a logical and age-appropriate sequence to give each student an opportunity to move forward in his or her faith. Such a plan will include the identification of a desired set of student outcomes, the selection of appropriate pedagogical strategies, and the use of quality resources to support the work.

Appendix 5

Sampling of Biblical References for Spiritual Formation

While Scripture is full of references to the need for each of us to be transformed into Christ's likeness, a few relevant passages are quoted below.

"You shall love the Lord your God with all your heart and with all your soul and with all your might. And these words that I command you today shall be on your heart. You shall teach them diligently to your children, and shall talk of them when you sit in your house, and when you walk by the way, and when you lie down, and when you rise. You shall bind them as a sign on your hand, and they shall be as frontlets between your eyes. You shall write them on the doorposts of your house and on your gates."
Deuteronomy 6:5–9

"Then Jesus told his disciples, 'If anyone would come after me, let him deny himself and take up his cross and follow me. For whoever would save his life will lose it, but whoever loses his life for my sake will find it. For what will it profit a man if he gains the whole world and forfeits his soul? Or what shall a man give in return for his soul? For the Son of Man is going to come with his angels in the glory of the Father, and then he will repay each person according to what he has done.'"
Matthew 16:24–27

"I appeal to you therefore, brothers, by the mercies of God, to present your bodies as a living sacrifice, holy and acceptable to God, which is your spiritual worship. Do not be conformed to this world, but be transformed by the renewing of your mind, that by testing you may discern what is the will of God, what is good and acceptable and perfect."
Romans 12:1–2

"Not that I have already obtained this or am already perfect, but I press on to make it my own, because Christ Jesus has made me his own. Brothers, I do not consider that I have made it my own. But one thing I do: forgetting what lies behind and straining forward to what lies ahead, I press on toward the goal for the prize of the upward call of God in Christ Jesus."
Philippians 3:12–14

"Put to death therefore what is earthly in you: sexual immorality, impurity, passion, evil desire, and covetousness, which is idolatry. On account of these the wrath of God is coming. In these you too once walked, when you were living in them. But now you must put them all away: anger, wrath, malice, slander, and obscene talk from your mouth. Do not lie to one another, seeing that you have put off the old self with its practices and have put on the new self, which is being renewed in knowledge after the image of its creator."
Colossians 3:5–10

"For the grace of God has appeared, bringing salvation for all people, training us to renounce ungodliness and worldly passions, and to live self-controlled, upright, and godly lives in the present age, waiting for our blessed hope, the appearing of the glory of our great God and Savior Jesus Christ, who gave himself for us to redeem us from all lawlessness and to purify for himself a people for his own possession who are zealous for good works."
Titus 2:11–14

Bibliography

PRIMARY SOURCES

Aristotle. *Nicomachean Ethics*. Translated by H. Rackham. Loeb Classical Library 73. Cambridge, MA: Harvard University Press, 1926.

Augustine. *Confessions: Books 9–13*. Edited and translated by Carolyn J.-B. Hammond. Loeb Classical Library 27. Cambridge, MA: Harvard University Press, 2016.

———. *On Christian Doctrine*. Translated by D. W. Robertson Jr. Library of Liberal Arts. Upper Saddle River, NJ: Prentice Hall, 1958.

Basil of Caesarea. "Address to Young Men, on How They Might Derive Benefit from Greek Literature." In *Basil: Letters 249–368, On Greek Literature*, translated by Roy J. Deferrari and Martin R. P. McGuire, 378–435. Loeb Classical Library 270. Cambridge, MA: Harvard University Press, 1934.

———. *On Social Justice*. Translated by C. Paul Schroeder. Popular Patristics 38. Crestwood, NY: St. Vladimir's Seminary Press, 2009.

Benedict of Nursia. *RB 1980—The Rule of St. Benedict in English*. Collegeville, MN: Liturgical, 1981.

Cassian, John. *The Conferences*. Translated by Boniface Ramsey. Ancient Christian Writers 57. Mahwah, NJ: Paulist, 1997.

Chrysostom, John. "Homily Twenty-One on the Epistle to the Ephesians." In *On Marriage and Family Life*, translated by David Anderson, 65–72. Popular Patristics 7. Crestwood, NY: St. Vladimir's Seminary Press, 1986.

———. *On the Incomprehensible Nature of God*. Translated by Paul W. Harkins. Fathers of the Church 72. Washington, DC: Catholic University of America Press, 1984.

———. "On Vainglory and the Right Way for Parents to Bring Up Their Children." In *Christianity and Pagan Culture in the Later Roman Empire: Together with an English Translation of John Chrysostom's Address on Vainglory and the Right Way for Parents to Bring Up Their Children*, translated by M. L. W. Laistner, 85–122. Ithaca, NY: Cornell University Press, 1967.

Cyril of Jerusalem. "The Procatechesis." In *Lectures on the Christian Sacraments*, translated by Maxwell E. Johnson, 64–83. Popular Patristics 57. Yonkers, NY: St. Vladimir's Seminary Press, 2017.

Gregory the Great. *The Book of Pastoral Rule*. Translated by George Demacopoulos. Popular Patristics 34. Crestwood, NY: St. Vladimir's Seminary Press, 2007.

———. *Dialogues*. Translated by Odo John Zimmerman. Fathers of the Church 39. Washington, DC: Catholic University of America Press, 1959.

Hippolytus of Rome. *On the Apostolic Tradition.* Translated by Alistair Stewart. Popular
    Patristics 22. Crestwood, NY: St. Vladimir's Seminary Press, 2001.
Justin Martyr. *The First and Second Apologies.* Translated by Leslie William Barnard.
    Ancient Christian Writers 56. New York: Paulist, 1997.
Lawrence, Brother. *The Practice of the Presence of God, with Spiritual Maxims.* Grand
    Rapids: Spire, 1958.
Plato. *Republic: Books 1–5.* Translated by Chris Emlyn-Jones and William Preddy. Loeb
    Classical Library 237. Cambridge, MA: Harvard University Press, 2013.

SECONDARY SOURCES

Anglican Church in North America, custodian. *The Book of Common Prayer and
    Administration of the Sacraments with Other Rites and Ceremonies of the Church,
    According to the Use of the Anglican Church in North America, Together with the
    New Coverdale Psalter.* Huntington Beach, CA: Anglican Liturgy, 2019.
Arnold, Clinton E. "Early Church Catechesis and New Christians' Classes in Contemporary
    Evangelicalism." *Journal of the Evangelical Theological Society* 47 (2004) 39–54.
Azadegan, Ebrahim. "Divine Hiddenness and Human Sin: The Noetic Effect of Sin."
    Journal of Reformed Theology 7 (2013) 69–90.
Badley, Ken. "Clarifying 'Faith-Learning Integration': Essentially Contested Concepts
    and the Concept-Conception Distinction." *Journal of Education and Christian
    Belief* 13 (2009) 7–17.
Bevins, Winfield. *Ever Ancient, Ever New: The Allure of Liturgy for a New Generation.*
    Grand Rapids: Zondervan, 2019.
———, and Kay Bevins. *Field Guide for Family Prayer.* Franklin, TN: Seedbed, 2019.
Black, Vicki K. *Welcome to the Church Year: An Introduction to the Seasons of the
    Episcopal Church.* Harrisburg, PA: Morehouse, 2004.
Boersma, Hans. *Seeing God: The Beatific Vision in Christian Tradition.* Grand Rapids:
    Eerdmans, 2018.
Bonhoeffer, Dietrich. *The Cost of Discipleship.* Translated by R. H. Fuller, revised by
    Imgard Booth. New York: Touchstone, 1995.
Bowler, Kate. *Blessed: A History of the American Prosperity Gospel.* Oxford: Oxford
    University Press, 2013.
Boyd, Jared Patrick. *Imaginative Prayer: A Yearlong Guide for Your Child's Spiritual
    Formation.* Downers Grove, IL: InterVarsity, 2017.
Brown, Peter. *The Rise of Western Christendom: Triumph and Diversity, A.D. 200–1000.*
    Rev. ed. Malden, MA: Wiley-Blackwell, 2013.
Bullis, Ronald K. "Applying St. Cyril's Pedagogy to Contemporary Christian Education."
    Christian Education Journal 15 (2018) 361–74.
Burton, Tara Isabella. *Strange Rites: New Religions for a Godless World.* New York:
    PublicAffairs, 2020.
Campbell, Joseph. *The Hero with a Thousand Faces.* 3rd ed. Novato, CA: New World
    Library, 2008.
Carnegie, Andrew. "The Gospel of Wealth." Carnegie Corporation of New York, June
    1889. https://www.carnegie.org/about/our-history/gospelofwealth.
Carr, Nicholas. *The Shallows: What the Internet Is Doing to Our Brains.* New York:
    Norton, 2011.

Chittister, Joan D. *Wisdom Distilled from the Daily: Living the Rule of St. Benedict Today.* New York: HarperOne, 1990.

Choung, James. *True Story: A Christianity Worth Believing In.* Downers Grove, IL: InterVarsity, 2008.

Christou, Theodore Michael. "Raising an Athlete for Christ: Saint John Chrysostom and Education in Byzantium." *Akropolis* 2 (2018) 105–18.

Conwell, Russell Herman. "Acres of Diamonds." American Rhetoric, 1890. https://www.americanrhetoric.com/speeches/rconwellacresofdiamonds.htm.

Crouch, Andy. *The Tech-Wise Family: Everyday Steps to Putting Technology in Its Proper Place.* Grand Rapids: Baker, 2017.

Deanesly, Margaret. *A History of the Medieval Church 590–1500.* 9th ed. London: Routledge, 1969.

Deferrari, Roy J. "Prefatory Note." In *Basil: Letters 249–368, On Greek Literature,* 365–76. Loeb Classical Library 270. Cambridge, MA: Harvard University Press, 1934.

Demacopoulos, George E. *Gregory the Great: Ascetic, Pastor, and First Man of Rome.* Notre Dame, IN: University of Notre Dame Press, 2015.

Demarest, Bruce. *Seasons of the Soul: Stages of Spiritual Development.* Downers Grove, IL: InterVarsity, 2009.

De Wet, Chris L. *Preaching Bondage: John Chrysostom and the Discourse of Slavery in Early Christianity.* Oakland, CA: University of California Press, 2015.

DeYoung, Rebecca Konyndyk. *Glittering Vices: A New Look at the Seven Deadly Sins and Their Remedies.* 2nd ed. Grand Rapids: Brazos, 2020.

Dreher, Rod. *The Benedict Option: A Strategy for Christians in a Post-Christian Nation.* New York: Sentinel, 2017.

———. *Live Not by Lies: A Manual for Christian Dissidents.* New York: Sentinel, 2020.

Evans, G. R. *The Thought of Gregory the Great.* Cambridge Studies in Medieval Life and Thought. Cambridge, UK: Cambridge University Press, 1986.

Ferguson, Kristen A. *Excellence in Online Education: Creating a Christian Community on Mission.* Nashville: B&H Academic, 2020.

Fitzgerald, F. Scott. *The Great Gatsby.* New York: Scribner, 2004.

Foster, Richard J. *Celebration of Discipline: The Path to Spiritual Growth.* 3rd ed. New York: HarperCollins, 1998.

Gaebelein, Frank E. *The Pattern of God's Truth: The Integration of Faith and Learning.* Colorado Springs: Association of Christian Schools International, 1954.

Garber, Stephen. *The Fabric of Faithfulness: Weaving Together Belief and Behavior.* Rev. ed. Downers Grove, IL: InterVarsity, 2007.

Glanzer, Perry L. "Why We Should Discard 'the Integration of Faith and Learning': Rearticulating the Mission of the Christian Scholar." *Journal of Education and Christian Belief* 12 (2008) 41–51.

González, Justo L. *The Story of Christianity.* 2 vols. Rev. ed. New York: HarperOne, 2010.

Grudem, Wayne. *Systematic Theology: An Introduction to Biblical Doctrine.* Grand Rapids: Zondervan, 1994.

Harmless, William. *Augustine and the Catechumenate.* Collegeville, MN: Liturgical, 1995.

Heath, Chip, and Dan Heath. *Made to Stick: Why Some Ideas Survive and Others Die.* Rev. ed. New York: Random House, 2008.

Hildebrand, Stephen M. *Basil of Caesarea.* Early Church Fathers. London: Routledge, 2018.

————. *The Trinitarian Theology of Basil of Caesarea: A Synthesis of Greek Thought and Biblical Truth*. Washington, DC: Catholic University of America Press, 2007.

Hill, Charles E. *Regnum Caelorum: Patterns of Millennial Thought in Early Christianity*. 2nd ed. Grand Rapids: Eerdmans, 2001.

Hill, Wesley. *The Lord's Prayer: A Guide to Praying to Our Father*. Christian Essentials. Bellingham, WA: Lexham, 2019.

Holder, Arthur Z. "Saint Basil the Great on Secular Education and Christian Virtue." *Religious Education* 87 (1992) 395–415.

Hughes, Kyle R. *How the Spirit Became God: The Mosaic of Early Christian Pneumatology*. Eugene, OR: Cascade, 2020.

Hull, John. "Aiming for Christian Education, Settling for Christians Educating: The Christian School's Replication of a Public School's Paradigm." *Christian Scholar's Review* 32 (2003) 203–23.

Jensen, Robin M. *Baptismal Imagery in Early Christianity: Ritual, Visual, and Theological Dimensions*. Grand Rapids: Baker Academic, 2012.

Johnson, Maxwell E. "Introduction." In *Lectures on the Christian Sacraments*, translated by Maxwell E. Johnson, 13–62. Popular Patristics 57. Yonkers, NY: St. Vladimir's Seminary Press, 2017.

Kalleres, Dayna S. "Cultivating True Sight at the Center of the World: Cyril of Jerusalem and the Lenten Catechumenate." *Church History* 74 (2005) 431–59.

Keener, Craig S. *Gift and Giver: The Holy Spirit for Today*. Grand Rapids: Baker Academic, 2001.

Kelly, J. N. D. *Golden Mouth: The Story of John Chrysostom—Ascetic, Preacher, Bishop*. Ithaca, NY: Cornell University Press, 1995.

Laistner, M. L. W. *Christianity and Pagan Culture in the Later Roman Empire: Together with an English Translation of John Chrysostom's* Address on Vainglory and the Right Way for Parents to Bring Up Their Children. Ithaca, NY: Cornell University Press, 1951.

Litfin, Bryan M. *Getting to Know the Church Fathers: An Evangelical Introduction*. Grand Rapids: Brazos, 2007.

Littlejohn, Robert, and Charles T. Evans. *Wisdom and Eloquence: A Christian Paradigm for Classical Learning*. Wheaton, IL: Crossway, 2006.

Louth, Andrew. *Introducing Eastern Orthodox Theology*. Downers Grove, IL: IVP Academic, 2013.

Louv, Richard. *Last Child in the Woods: Saving Our Children from Nature-Deficit Disorder*. Rev. ed. New York: Workman, 2008.

Macchia, Stephen A. *Crafting a Rule of Life: An Invitation to the Well-Ordered Way*. Downers Grove, IL: InterVarsity, 2012.

MacIntyre, Alasdair C. *After Virtue: A Study in Moral Theory*. 3rd ed. Notre Dame, IN: University of Notre Dame Press, 2007.

Mamalakis, Philip. *Parenting toward the Kingdom: Orthodox Principles of Child-Rearing*. Chesterton, IN: Ancient Faith Publishing, 2016.

Markus, R. A. *Gregory the Great and His World*. Cambridge, UK: Cambridge University Press, 1997.

Mayer, Wendy, and Pauline Allen. *John Chrysostom*. Early Church Fathers. London: Routledge, 2000.

McCaulley, Esau. *Reading While Black: African American Biblical Interpretation as an Exercise in Hope*. Downers Grove, IL: IVP Academic, 2020.

McGowan, Andrew B. *Ancient Christian Worship: Early Church Practices in Social, Historical, and Theological Perspective*. Grand Rapids: Baker Academic, 2014.

Moo, Douglas J., and Jonathan A. Moo. *Creation Care: A Biblical Theology of the Natural World*. Biblical Theology for Life. Grand Rapids: Zondervan, 2018.

O'Donohue, John. *Anam Ċara: A Book of Celtic Wisdom*. New York: HarperCollins, 1997.

Okholm, Dennis. *Dangerous Passions, Deadly Sins: Learning from the Psychology of Ancient Monks*. Grand Rapids: Brazos, 2014.

———. *Learning Theology through the Church's Worship: An Introduction to Christian Belief*. Grand Rapids: Baker Academic, 2018.

Ortlund, Gavin. *Theological Retrieval for Evangelicals: Why We Need Our Past to Have a Future*. Wheaton, IL: Crossway, 2019.

Packer, J. I., and Gary A. Parrett. *Grounded in the Gospel: Building Believers the Old-Fashioned Way*. Grand Rapids: Baker, 2010.

Packer, J. I., and Joel Scandrett, eds. *To Be a Christian: An Anglican Catechism*. Wheaton, IL: Crossway, 2020.

Palmer, Parker J. *The Courage to Teach: Exploring the Inner Landscape of a Teacher's Life*. 3rd ed. San Francisco: Jossey-Bass, 2017.

———. *To Know as We Are Known: Education as a Spiritual Journey*. New York: HarperOne, 1983.

Paris, Jenell. *Teach from the Heart: Pedagogy as Spiritual Practice*. Eugene, OR: Cascade, 2016.

Pazmiño, Robert W. *Foundational Issues in Christian Education: An Introduction in Evangelical Perspective*. 3rd ed. Grand Rapids: Baker Academic, 2008.

Peters, Greg. *The Monkhood of All Believers: The Monastic Foundation of Christian Spirituality*. Grand Rapids: Baker Academic, 2018.

Peterson, Eugene H. *The Contemplative Pastor: Returning to the Art of Spiritual Direction*. Grand Rapids: Eerdmans, 1989.

———. *Eat This Book: A Conversation in the Art of Spiritual Reading*. Grand Rapids: Eerdmans, 2006.

———. *Under the Unpredictable Plant: An Exploration in Vocational Holiness*. Grand Rapids: Eerdmans, 1992.

Pfatteicher, Philip H. *Journey into the Heart of God: Living the Liturgical Year*. Oxford: Oxford University Press, 2013.

Postman, Neil. *Technopoly: The Surrender of Culture to Technology*. New York: Knopf, 1992.

Powell, Kara, and Chap Clark. *Sticky Faith: Everyday Ideas to Build Lasting Faith in Your Kids*. Grand Rapids: Zondervan, 2011.

Purves, Andrew. *Pastoral Theology in the Classical Tradition*. Louisville: Westminster John Knox, 2001.

Raab, Christian. "Gregory, Marmion, Merton, and Louf: Insights from the Benedictine Religious Family for the Practice of Spiritual Direction." In *A Science of the Saints: Studies in Spiritual Direction*, edited by Robert E. Alvis, 24–52. Collegeville, MN: Liturgical, 2020.

Rapp, Claudia. *Holy Bishops in Late Antiquity: The Nature of Christian Leadership in an Age of Transition*. Berkeley, CA: University of California Press, 2005.

Rylaarsdam, David. *John Chrysostom on Divine Pedagogy: The Coherence of His Theology and Preaching*. Oxford Early Christian Studies. Oxford: Oxford University Press, 2014.

Scazzero, Peter. *Emotionally Healthy Spirituality*. Rev. ed. Grand Rapids: Zondervan, 2017.

Schroeder, C. Paul. "Introduction." In *On Social Justice*, translated by C. Paul Schroeder, 15–39. Popular Patristics 38. Crestwood, NY: St. Vladimir's Seminary Press, 2009.

Schütz, Christian. "To Serve Life: The Rule of Benedict as a Guide for a Benedictine School." *American Benedictine Review* 60 (2009) 154–67.

Senkbeil, Harold L. *The Care of Souls: Cultivating a Pastor's Heart*. Bellingham, WA: Lexham, 2019.

Sittser, Gerald L. *Resilient Faith: How the Early Christian "Third Way" Changed the World*. Grand Rapids: Brazos, 2019.

Smith, Christian, and Melinda Lundquist Denton. *Soul Searching: The Religious and Spiritual Lives of American Teenagers*. Oxford: Oxford University Press, 2005.

Smith, David I. *On Christian Teaching: Practicing Faith in the Classroom*. Grand Rapids: Eerdmans, 2018.

———, and Barbara Carvill. *The Gift of the Stranger: Faith, Hospitality, and Foreign Language Learning*. Grand Rapids: Eerdmans, 2000.

———, and Susan M. Felch. *Teaching and Christian Imagination*. Grand Rapids: Eerdmans, 2016.

———, et al. *Digital Life Together: The Challenge of Technology for Christian Schools*. Grand Rapids: Eerdmans, 2020.

Smith, James K. A. *Desiring the Kingdom: Worship, Worldview, and Cultural Formation*. Vol. 1 of *Cultural Liturgies*. Grand Rapids: Baker Academic, 2009.

Taylor, Charles. *A Secular Age*. Cambridge, MA: Belknap Press of Harvard University Press, 2007.

Thornton, Martin. *English Spirituality: An Outline of Ascetical Theology according to the English Pastoral Tradition*. 1986. Reprint, Eugene, OR: Wipf & Stock, 2012.

"Throughlines." Teaching for Transformation. https://www.teachingfortransformation.org/our-approach/core-practices/throughlines.

Trentham, John David. "Reading the Social Sciences Theologically (Part 1): Approaching and Qualifying Models of Human Development." *Christian Education Journal* 16 (2019) 458–75.

———. "Reading the Social Sciences Theologically (Part 2): Engaging and Appropriating Models of Human Development." *Christian Education Journal* 16 (2019) 476–94.

Trueman, Carl R. *The Rise and Triumph of the Modern Self: Cultural Amnesia, Expressive Individualism, and the Road to Sexual Revolution*. Wheaton, IL: Crossway, 2020.

Vanderstelt, Jeff. *Gospel Fluency: Speaking the Truths of Jesus into the Everyday Stuff of Life*. Wheaton, IL: Crossway, 2017.

Vandici, Gratian. "Reading the Rules of Knowledge in the Story of the Fall: Calvin and Reformed Epistemology on the Noetic Effects of Original Sin." *Journal of Theological Interpretation* 10 (2016) 173–91.

Waal, Esther de. *Seeking God: The Way of St. Benedict*. 2nd ed. Collegeville, MN: Liturgical, 2001.

Wallace, Carey. *Stories of the Saints: Bold and Inspiring Tales of Adventure, Grace, and Courage*. Illustrated by Nick Thornborrow. New York: Workman, 2020.

Warner, Larry. *Journey with Jesus: Discovering the Spiritual Exercises of Saint Ignatius.* Downers Grove, IL: InterVarsity, 2010.

Warren, Tish Harrison. *Liturgy of the Ordinary: Sacred Practices in Everyday Life.* Downers Grove, IL: InterVarsity, 2016.

White, Carolinne. "Introduction." In *The Rule of St. Benedict*, vii–xxxii. Penguin Classics. London: Penguin, 2008.

Wigger, J. Bradley. *Together We Pray: A Prayer Book for Families.* St. Louis: Chalice, 2005.

Willard, Dallas. *Renovation of the Heart: Putting on the Character of Christ.* Rev. ed. Colorado Springs: NavPress, 2012.

Williams, D. H. *Evangelicals and Tradition: The Formative Influence of the Early Church.* Evangelical *Ressourcement*: Ancient Sources for the Church's Future. Grand Rapids: Baker Academic, 2005.

Williams, Thaddeus J. *Confronting Injustice without Compromising Truth: Twelve Questions Christians Should Ask about Social Justice.* Grand Rapids: Zondervan Academic, 2020.

Wright, N. T. *Surprised by Hope: Rethinking Heaven, the Resurrection, and the Mission of the Church.* New York: HarperOne, 2008.

Yaconelli, Mark. *Contemplative Youth Ministry: Practicing the Presence of Jesus.* Youth Specialties. Grand Rapids: Zondervan, 2006.

Yarnold, Edward. *Cyril of Jerusalem.* Early Church Fathers. London: Routledge, 2000.

Young, Frances M. *Biblical Exegesis and the Formation of Christian Culture.* Cambridge, UK: Cambridge University Press, 1997.

Ancient Document Index

Index of Names and Subjects

Made in United States
North Haven, CT
28 May 2024

53050477R00125